Everything About Me Is Fake... and I'm Perfect!

ALSO BY JANICE DICKINSON

No Lifeguard on Duty

Everything About Me Is Fake... and I'm Perfect!

JANICE DICKINSON

HARPER

NEW YORK • LONDON • TORONTO • SYDNEY

All photographs are courtesy of Janice Dickinson except:

Text: Photographs on pages 18 and 53 by Albert Watson; photograph on page 67 by Larry Hammerness; photograph on page 166 by Harry Langdon; photographs on pages 178 and 231 by Phillip Dixon; photograph on page 228 by Kenneth Babolcsay; photograph on page 248 by Mark Giard.

Insert: Photographs on pages 1, 5 (bottom left and far right), 9 (top left and bottom) by Albert Watson; photographs on pages 2, 3 (bottom), 6 (bottom) © by Richard Avedon; photograph on page 3 (top) by Patrick Demarchelier; photograph on page 4 by Mitchel Gray; photographs on pages 5 (top left), 6 (top) by Francesco Scavullo; photographs on page 7 (top and bottom) by Harry Langdon; photograph on page 8 by Sante D'Orazio; photograph on page 9 (top right) by Phillip Dixon; photographs on pages 12, 14 (bottom left and right) by Isabel Snyder; photographs on pages 13, 14 (top), 16 (bottom left) by Mark Giard; photograph on page 15 by Nick Knight.

A hardcover edition of this book was published in 2004 by ReganBooks, an imprint of HarperCollins Publishers.

HarperCollins books may be purchased for educational, business, or sales promotional use. For information please write: Special Markets Department, HarperCollins Publishers Inc., 10 East 53rd Street, New York, NY 10022.

FIRST PAPERBACK EDITION PUBLISHED 2005.

Designed by Kris Tobiassen

The Library of Congress has catalogued the hardcover edition as follows:

Dickinson, Janice, 1955–
    Everything about me is fake . . . and I'm perfect / Janice Dickinson. 1st ed.
      xii, 260p. : ill. (some col.); 24 cm.
    0-06-055469-X (hbk. : alk. paper)
    0-06-055470-3 (mass market)
    Includes index.
    1. Dickinson, Janice, 1955– 2. Beauty, Personal 3. Models (Persons) —United States—Biography.
    RA778.D38 2004
    646.7 / 042 22

ISBN 13: 978-0-06-055470-5 (pbk)

ISBN 10: 0-06-055470-3 (pbk)

08 09 WBC/RRD 10 9 8 7 6 5 4

To Savvy and Nathan,
the hilarious, astonishing, amazing creations that God has bestowed upon me—
thank you for the privilege of being your mother

Contents

Acknowledgments

Thank you to all those involved with the making of *Everything About Me Is Fake . . . and I'm Perfect*—without your patience, generosity, and talent, book number two would never have been possible. To:

Rip Mason. You are the best and the brightest. Don't forget it.

Alexis, Mitch, and Morgan Mayer.

Debbie and Evan.

Simon and Melanie Fields.

Graham Kaye and Rodney from Creative Management for all their tireless efforts.

Yatti and Joe Ratna.

Marc Jacobson, my partner in crime and in makeup. My luck shifted the moment you picked up the phone. I owe you a world of gratitude forever. Thank you for being tenacious, brilliant, and superb.

My brother, Edward Tricome—you simply rule.

Elizabeth, for everything.

Cindy Pearlman. Without running in Manolo Blahniks on our hikes, we wouldn't have developed our corns. You are truly the Black Pearl of the sea.

Alissa LeViness, for she knew not what she embarked on when the other editors paled in her shadow. Thank you for your tireless effort on book number two of the trilogy. Ay, Mami!

The Yoda Master himself, Cal Morgan, the greatest editor and my friend.

My co-alpha dawg, Judith Regan, who sees all and knows all. Thank you for believing once again in the mission.

Paul Olsewski and Carl Raymond, also sex symbols in their own right. Where would I be without the Boy Wonders of the industry? You guys rock so hard!

Angelica Canales—thank you!

Mark Kesten and Duke. You guys are two, hot stud muffins.

John Branca, Wendy Heller, and Matt Johnson—the most talented fine print artists of all time. Thank you for all your help.

Buck Lockwood, the Tuscan Baseball Cowboy, for belief.

Much gratitude to the United Talent Agency—you are all fabulous and incredibly intuitive, especially Itay Reiss and Lee Horowitz. Thank you for having the intuitive instinct for recognizing true talent (moi)!

Greg Mayday and Guy Macalwayne at Universal, for depositing my model story seed in the first place, and thank you, also, Larry Thompson, for believing in the project. Merci! Gracias! Danke schön! You are the men of power that truly rock—thank you all for everything.

Jim Fox and Mark Jackson. Thank you for cleaning up my act.

John Pearson, for always being right.

Dr. Uzzy and his devoted wife, Yael Reiss, for the balance of anti-aging. Long may *you* live!

Joe, Betty, Rosa, and the entire staff of the Beverly-Glen Market. You are the family I never knew. Thank you for taking me in always.

John Peters, my big brother, always watching. You're the best.

Warner Avenue Elementary School. Savvy's lineup requires great gratitude. Thank you: Rhonda Peyton, Nicky Peoples, Ms. Saunders, Louise Kirshner, Mr. Kaufman, Mr. Crosley, Lori Terada, Evan Brown, Beryl, Mark Madsen, Ms. Burr, Ms. McCloud, Ms. Gowit. Savvy's extraordinary teachers—thank you for molding her brain.

Coach Keith and everyone at the Warner Star Program, especially Vicki Feldman and Elissa Spearling. Thank you for your tireless efforts.

Oded Bahat, my sexy, hot, superlative, hot, sex symbol extraordinaire, my periodontist.

Irene Marisolav. To the hottest hygienist who ever rocked teeth, I love you. Sorry about the appointments—I must have been in bed!

Aida Thibiant—for formulating the best skincare products I've ever used—their products are amazing.

Neil Lane—superstar jewelry legend extraordinaire—thank you for your generosity and patience in jewelry. God bless you forever.

Dr. Tom Manero, from the Pain Relief Center, you are the greatest chiropractor that ever walked the earth. Thank you for everything.

David Gray at the Equinox Gym in West Hollywood.

Katie Wagner.

Sharon Osbourne.

To the entire staff of the Beverly-Glen Deli: Karen, Nate, Jorge, Barry, and Loretta. The salamis aren't the only thing hangin' at the deli!

Beverly Hills Nail Design, the Prid-da Salon, and the Cristoph Salon in Beverly Hills.

To Cheri, Kobe, Evan Skyler, and Ryan Haskett—Savvy's second family. Without you, I'm nothing. Thank you.

The Chazanas Clan. West Wanda is a better place knowing you're there.

My neighbor Peter, my second story man extraordinaire!

Mr. Liam. It would have been death for the first book without your kickstart.

Jimmy Rip and Tony Peck, once again, the giants of guiding my star to sobriety.

Steve Bing, for just being cool.

All of my friends in AA. Your struggles and sanctuary keep me sober one day at a time. All of my gratitude. Thank you.

My sponsor, Sabrina. I love you.

Rita, Flora, Asha, and Coco. I love you. Long live the girls!

Mona & Co. The best designer I know.

Diane von Furstenberg and her entire staff. Much gratitude for the flirty dresses.

Eric Nicholson, Valente, and Renee. Thank you for all your assistance in styling, hair, and makeup on *America's Next Top Model*.

Nigel Barker and his lovely wife.

The Diva, Tyra Banks, the last of the breed Supermodel. All of my gratitude and love.

Ken Mock—Mr. Do-it! THANK YOU! THANK YOU! THANK YOU!

Dana Gabron, Anthony, and the crew of *America's Next Top Model*.

Les Moonvess at CBS. You rock! Anyone else I forgot on the show—sorry, but thank you!

Michael Birnbaum.

Julie and Joe Watson.

Linda Michael.

Joel and Eileen Birnbaum and their family.

And my readers—this is book number two of the trilogy. I am the *Lord of the Rings* of supermodels, so please look forward to book number three. Oh yeah! Ay, Mami!

Last, but not least, in loving memory of Connie Tricome—just plainly and simply the best there ever was. May you rest in peace.

Perfliction

"Deliver me from reasons why you'd rather cry. I'd rather fly."
— THE DOORS

Hollywood, California, March 1994. For the safety of the general public, there ought to be a sign on my ass reading Caution — Extra-Wide Load. When I sit down, it registers a 6.0 on the Richter. Luckily this is Los Angeles, where we're obsessed with the earth actually moving . . . and no, I'm not getting to my sex life in the first paragraph of this book. (You'll have to read at least three or four more lines until we get there.)

Back to my bod. It's humongous, gargantuan, Orca-like — which is not how the world's first supermodel (me) likes to describe herself in print, but I have to be honest. I'm so big I wonder if I'll wind up on CNN: "Janice Dickinson plopped down on a couch today, forcing hundreds of people to run for cover in doorways."

I'm eight months pregnant, eighty pounds overweight, and I'm going out of my mind. For the first time in my life, I let it all go and did something insane: I picked up a fork and ate, which is strictly forbidden when you're the world's first supermodel. For eight months, there was also no binging, no purging, no cocaine, and no alcohol. My drug of choice was food: I was mainlining Hostess and Snickers. I ate like a heifer, looked like an elephant, and dressed like a blimp in a man's white overshirt and black pants.

I'm waddling through the lobby of the ultra-chichi, totally fabulous Odeon restaurant with my soon-to-be-ex-husband, Simon Fields. And that's when I happen to see my former lover walk through the door, glance my way, and ignore me completely.

That's Mick Jagger's love for you.

I stare hard at him, wanting a little satisfaction, but I can't get no . . . well, you know. Mick looks startled by my intense glare—and the fact that I mutter loudly, "My God, they'll let anybody in here."

Ah, the lightbulb moment that follows. He clearly recognizes my voice, but when you've met so many women and fucked so many people, it takes a minute to process who's who on the horizontal food chain. Meanwhile, I'm seething, burning, exploding—and Mick deserves my wrath. The nerve of him, dismissing me as if figuring which decade he did me is just too much bother tonight. (I can just about see a faint question mark lingering on his face: "Did I actually go through a period of fat chicks?")

I slept with Mick for the better part of a year. In fact, there came a point when I couldn't get rid of this annoying megastar; I once described him to my girlfriends as "the most famous unwanted guest." Frankly, I wasn't that into him, and in hindsight I'm fairly certain the only reason I stayed was to tell my grandchildren that I'd slept with a Rolling Stone. Yet I know Mick was into me, in more ways than one.

In that affected English accent, he kept begging me, "Baby, I want you to have my baby." When I ignored his mood to multiply (imagine the lips on *that* kid!), he switched tactics and started sending me huge pink elephant roses, signing the card, "I love you. Prince Philip. Meet me in the lobby right now. I'm at your hotel."

Jerry Hall? Jerry who?

Around the six-month mark, something happened in our little affair that made things very tricky. I got swept up in the private jets, the fast lane, and the free tickets to the shows. Who wouldn't? So what if he wasn't a Greek god—this man knew how to seduce a woman. He knew how to love me.

Eventually we broke up, and afterward I never expected to be on his Christmas card list again. I did think, however, I might warrant a simple nod or hello if we ever met again in public. I wasn't expecting to be defeated and deflated—in other words, snubbed.

Here is how it goes: Mick runs his hand through his long hair, glances at a few women at the bar who might be good for dessert, eyeballs me for one second, and then brushes past looking for greener pastures. After all, I'm no longer a ninety-five-pound pixie waif with short hair and no breasts. I didn't look like a hot little boy anymore, which is the way he seemed to like his women, or at least the way he seemed to like me.

No wonder he named his first child Jade. He's so *jaded.*

At this point, I start to fume and spew out the following under my breath: "Son-of-a-bitch-asshole-mother*fucker.* Does he think he can fuck me and just turn around? You weren't that good anyway!" As for Simon, he appears, well, *uncomfortable.* "Janice," he whispers. "Bloody hell. Let it go!"

Blame it on the hormones. Or on the fact that Ms. Janice Dickinson is no longer perfect. Four weeks shy of giving birth, I can't even fake it. Boobs hanging, face swollen, belly protruding, sucking in my gut—what's the point?

A few minutes later, the biggest rock star on the planet is standing smack in front of me, a pregnant girl now so immersed in her menu that she pretends not to notice the only man on the planet with lips bigger than her own. The vibe is so thick you can feel the glass wall I've erected between us.

"*Janice.* I can't believe it's really *you,*" Mick says. But it's hard for him to hide his look of amazement, mixed with a little disgust.

Yes, it's finally dawned on Mick that he used to sleep with me—or some thinner, more supermodel-like edition of me he used to know. You'd think Mick had never seen a pregnant woman in his life—as if the tour bus had somehow taken him to some foreign planet where the women have hips that don't fit in size-0 jeans. In fact, Mick is so amazed I'm this big that he gives me a head-to-toe appraisal (no, he won't be inviting me home). Then, I swear, one of his huge lips unravels so far forward that the restaurant has to send two model-like attendant boys to return it from the parking lot.

My brain screams, *Who the fuck does he think he is not to recognize me? Even if I do look like Jabba the Hutt . . .*

I pause, glance around the room, and execute a 10.0 hair flip.

"So, Mick," I say in my kindest voice. "I guess they'll let *any*one in this restaurant."

"I just can't believe it's you," Mick repeats, stunned. All I can think is, *I look like I ought to have an apple in my mouth and a spit running through my back.*

"Why can't you believe it? I'm *pregnant*, Mick," I say, spitting venom. I can't believe that at one time I actually thought I was in love with this guy. I mean, he was so sensitive he once dedicated "Let It Bleed" to me at a Stones concert as an ode to my period.

Speaking of hormonal, I was feeling a little more that way every minute. "Don't worry, Mick. It's not like I'm packing boxes at a Twinkie warehouse and sampling the goods."

Mick can't discriminate. Fat to him is fat. Bulge on my hips, no bulge in his pants.

And he's not the only one. In this town, you can't be a piece of ass if you've got a fat ass. And so it goes. Here is a man who sent me a basket of caviar and flowers when I was in rehab in 1982, who filled my hotel rooms with roses at $200 a dozen back in the day. I couldn't have been a meaner bitch to him back then, but in his eyes I could do no wrong. Now it's a different story.

That was ages ago. A few years later, I had a beautiful baby boy named Nathan, and now he's sixteen. A year ago, he turned to size-4 me and said, "Mom, you're getting a little fat." (He knows that bothers me more than an unclean room or stealing the car keys.) A few years after

Nathan, I had a gorgeous daughter named Savvy, and now *she* thinks she's getting a little too heavy. She's ten.

My little girl knows the difference between egg whites and yolks. After all, she was weaned on MET-Rx and PowerBars. She knows I've had my tits done twice, and the amount of botulism (sorry, Botox) I'm packing in my face could wipe out several small European countries.

These days a girl has to work it so the Jaggers, the jagoffs, and everyone in between will get what they want—and she gets what she needs.

That's why everything about me is fake . . . and I'm perfect. Do I have any other choice?

That's society's love for you.

There's a reason I decided to write a second book, a follow-up to *No Lifeguard on Duty*. In a nutshell, I wanted to demystify the concept of being perfect, which in a few words is *a load of crap*. I know what you're thinking: it'd be easier to stomach that message if it weren't coming from a supermodel. But think about that for a minute: do you really want the world's most heinous troll telling you that being all that isn't . . . *all that?* It takes a supermodel to pull back the curtain and show you Oz isn't all it was cracked up to be.

This book is about ripping off the designer clothes, washing off the makeup, letting the rest of the mascara run, and stripping away all the layers that created my life as a photo shoot.

If I know only one thing, it's that perfection is the ultimate addiction. To paraphrase the admission statement of that well-known support group, my name is Janice and I'm a perfection addict. My disease? I call it *perfliction*. It's classified in medical journals as the extreme need to be more perfect than is humanly possible. My perfliction resulted in a four-decades-long struggle for sanity, starting with my childhood and zooming in on my long nights and days of modelmania.

Back in the day—as I love to refer to my supermodeldom—I appeared to be living the lifestyle of a character right out of Jackie Collins. But for me it was all very real. There were money, men, mansions, and more—much more than a girl deserves. Who was this girl, anyway? For those of you who have never met me, I was just your average too-skinny, too-tall, looked-like-a-boy, vulnerable, nervous, winging-it girl from Hollywood, Florida, who took all the shitty things life had to offer (including a pedophile for a father) and turned it into something pretty great. My drive was darn perfect, but my aim left something to be desired.

Speaking of desire, I was the It Girl before there was a new one every hour. My image graced the pages of *Vogue, Mademoiselle,* and *Harper's Bazaar,* and all the top photographers from A to W—Avedon to Weber—wanted to work with me. How I got in front of their lenses was anything but pretty, because beauty is an ugly business. That era was a buffet of surgery, puking, drugs, booze, and moments so horrifying that just remembering them for these pages is sure to give me a few wrinkles.

My fame (or maybe it was my face) got me dates with men who go by last names only—Stallone, Beatty, and Nicholson, for a start. But you know what? The troubles these men gave me—well, it wasn't so different from the crap I'm sure you've taken from a shithead boyfriend at one time or another. Only your man just wanted his CDs back; Stallone took back a half-million-dollar painting, a few Bvlgari diamonds, a bagel toaster, and a twelve-pack of Diet Coke. (If I live to be 100, I'll never figure out why he couldn't sell the painting and order in all the toast and Tab he wanted.) I had to learn the hard way that even famous men aren't enough to make a girl happy. It's really about what's on the inside. That's the most imperfect part of all of us, and often the most beautiful.

Cut to the here and now. I'm just as vulnerable to perfliction as anybody because the kind of dream life we're fed by the media is quite simply unattainable. Yet I know so many great women who won't let happiness enter their lives because they're reaching for the kind of image I used to sell. And the buyers are still lined up from coast to coast because we're *all* perflicted.

Well, now I want to put that image away and paint the real picture. I want to tell the truth because it's important to women out there, and to young girls like my ten-year-old Savvy, who is already growing up chased by the need to be someone or something else. These girls grow up into young women who want to live their lives inside the pages of a fashion magazine. I admire their innocence, laced as it is with hunger. To me these girls are like yearlings, ready to break out of the gates like I did when I was younger. But how many will make it in this perfection game?

When a young woman today tells me she wants to be a model, my advice is simple: "Go work at Hertz Rent-a-Car. Get a job at Wal-Mart. Do something else." I'm brutally honest because the modeling business is brutal—period. I love that these girls have dreams in their eyes, but it makes me sad when I think about how far they'll have to go—and no matter how far that is, it probably won't be far enough. I know because I've been there. I was just looking out from the other side, but now I'll take you on the inside.

Warning: This book is a cautionary tale about chasing something that's not within reach. It's for every woman who has ever stared at the strappy little numbers held up by those Victoria's Secret models and thought, "I wish that could be me." Chances are that can never be you, unless you have breast implants and then tape your boobs together inside the dress, only later to have them digitally enhanced by a nerd sitting at a computer screen. That's the image corporate America is selling and we're buying as a lifestyle.

What I've learned, through the years and tears, is that no one is perfect. But I *can* tell you how to raise the bar when it comes to diet, exercise, men, beauty, and everything else. This book may tone your flabby arms; more to the point, it'll firm up your flabby notions about beauty. Together we'll strive to become as good as possible, as perfect as we can be, without losing our minds. I'll tell you how to look great and feel even better.

Rule number one: Fake it until you make it. Act good until you *are* good. Practice confidence until you're confident, be patient even when it's killing you, consider yourself interesting until you truly believe you are, and eventually you won't be faking it anymore—you'll be living it.

The fakery for me began at the tender age of six, when my completely-in-denial mother sent me to kindergarten at the Little Flower Catholic School.

Sister No Sense of Humor couldn't have given a shit less about me having paper and crayons on the first day of school. She didn't even fret about the basic worries, like teaching me to read or saving my soul from God only knows what at that age. No, these sistas had bigger worries, starting with exactly how much leg a six-year-old could flash in the name of common decency. It was bound to be that kind of trouble because I grew up in South Florida. It's not like they were worried about frostbite.

Confidence rocks!

This was serious business. I'm half convinced these nuns must have been reading *Vogue* in the john or something, the way they obsessed with fashion—that is, skirt lengths.

On the first day of school little Janice excused herself to go pee, but it was really just my own attempt at youth perfection. In the john, I rolled my skirt to proper micromini length. Hell, I was upset that my little Mary Janes weren't platform shoes, but what could I do? I couldn't afford stilettos just yet, plus how could I pedal my Schwinn in them? Practical, I was. At least back then.

The minute I came out of the john looking much more of the moment, I felt myself yanked into the corner. Sister Child Abuser took one look at my naked legs, pulled a ruler out from I don't know where (use your imagination), and whacked the hell out of the backs of my tiny palms. Imagine, whacking a six-year-old for good fashion sense! I blame our conformity on the Catholic Church. (Save your cards and letters—I'm not changing my mind about this one.)

Life was giving me a good beating back then. At the time, I was being battered by my father for not conforming to his idea of parenting, which was to have sex with your children. (Talk about being reminded you're not perfect: when I told him to keep his dick to himself, my father screamed, "You should have been born a boy!") My mother beat me for not obeying the rules of our soul-crushing home and this ass-backwards school. The neighborhood bully roughed me up for fun, and now I had a nun on my ass.

So, yes, by age six, while other children were developing their math and language skills, I was sharpening up my acerbic wit and my judgmental, in-the-hood, don't-fuck-with-me attitude. Unfortunately, they didn't give grades for that kind of thing at the Little Flower School. Reading: C. Music: B. Won't Be Shit on by Others: A+! (Incidentally, which one do you think helped me the most as an adult woman in Hollywood or on runways all over the world?)

My attitude was just nature's way. I believe it's called *fight or flight*. I lived with my fists up.

But back to the nuns. I remember standing at the blackboard in front of the class, trying to do fractions. Each time I got one wrong, the nuns would smash my head into the blackboard. It hurt, but there were deeper concerns. "Hey, Sister, watch it—you're getting chalk in my pores!" I cried. That night I went home and borrowed my mother's exfoliating cream and studied harder. I just couldn't risk a breakout.

One day, one of the nicer sisters sat me down and told me, "Janice, you need to conform to society's norms." I gave her a blank stare, like I had no idea what she was talking about, but deep down I knew exactly where this little pep talk was going.

"We want to teach you to be a perfect little girl," she said, and as I inched forward in my seat, my skirt hiked up about three inches. The nun took one look at my emerging knees and got out the ruler. Busted! Bruised!

Could I sue?

Even my hairstyles were too seductive for these nuns. In second grade I used to love wearing my hair on the very top of my head, a spray of locks coming down like branches on a palm tree. The nuns made me take that down, too. Was I disheartened? Hell, no. I just went home, heisted my mother's purse, and painted my teeny-tiny nails bitch red.

My mother wore this beautiful deep red lipstick, just like Scarlett O'Hara. I used to sit and watch her apply it in this gorgeous way with a lip brush. She reminded me of a 1940s movie star. In a covert mission before the bus picked me up for school, I'd keep one eye out for my father while sneaking into my parents' bedroom, which wasn't exactly the safest area in our house given my father's extracurricular activities. If I made it to my mother's vanity, I'd smudge crimson lipstick on my mouth to make it look like I was sucking on cherry pits all day long. Strange, but even back then I knew the power of the mouth. I also knew how to look like a Kabuki princess.

"Janice, you wipe that sinful red paint off your mouth," the nuns would scream. "Do you want to go to Hell?"

How could I? I wanted to respond. I was already there.

———————————

At this point, I thought I might take my quest for perfection to a higher level. I'd start asking pertinent questions about our world, to help me begin to develop a perfect mind and heart. My first question to the nuns: *Why is Jesus in a diaper on the cross?* I was put in the corner. The nuns couldn't answer my question because they didn't *know.* Being a naturally inquisitive child, I didn't let my quest for a higher truth die. What is the Immaculate Conception? I asked. *Whack!* What's a virgin? *Whack!*

For God's sake, we couldn't talk about sex. Hello! I was the type of kid where if you couldn't talk about it, then I was Little Miss Curiosity times one hundred. I knew I'd figure it out in my own way. And thus began my career in voyeurism—which before long included peeping into my neighbors' windows. By that time I was about ten, and I noticed that the people who seemed so conservative when they were out grilling a steak, washing their car, or yelling at kids to stay off their lawn were actually porn stars in private. They were always fucking in the shower, which made them either very clean or very dirty, depending on your point of view.

My typical diary entry from the time:

Dear Diary,

As usual, some of my neighbors are going at it 24-7. I think she has fake tits. I also watched both of them get each other off. I'll write more tomorrow—I have algebra homework.

On certain nights, when the weather cooled off, I thought about bringing a barrel of popcorn to my hiding spot where I sat and peeped at them: this was better than any late-night movie I wasn't supposed to watch. I should have printed tickets and set up a concession stand in the bushes—between the acts of love I could have served "Janice's Snacks of Love." If I'd had access to a supplier for Junior Mints and Red Vines, I could have become a millionaire.

For me, watching the neighbors have sex was certainly better than listening to my parents fight, or watching the tube with my zoned-out mother. On TV, you never saw Gilligan bend Ginger over a straw bed. There were no blow jobs for Mary Tyler Moore because what if the guy messed up that bubble-helmet hair? Of course, you couldn't blame her for being so celibate; after all, who was she going to *do*, Mr. Grant? *Murray?* My neighbors, on the other hand? They seemed perfect for each other. Of course, there was always a chance she was faking it. I was too young to know the difference.

The peeping-Tammy act was only one way I wasn't like other kids. I also bucked the norm in my own family. By the age of eleven I'd convinced my mother that I'd had enough of nuns, and that she had no choice but to get me out of those ugly blue uniforms, which would have added fat rolls to anyone's hips. I insisted that she enroll me in good ol' regular junior high school, where I could dress like a human being.

The perks of "normal" school were unbelievable. Forget those boring little navy blue uniforms. I started wearing lowrise hip-hugger jeans to school. I was working those pants before most of today's fashion designers had pubic hair.

And as I got older, I began to notice something funny: I wasn't the only one interested in my advanced sense of style. Men were beginning to notice that I was a perfect specimen. And, frankly, I was a little bit too familiar with those kinds of looks already: my dad was a leering virtuoso.

Let's rewind one more time . . .

The first person who got me agonizing over being perfect was my father, the pedophile. The rat bastard took one look at his not-even-close-to-okay daughter, and suddenly I was convinced something was wrong with me. Sure, I was a girl; nobody's perfect. But there wasn't much I could do to change it—short of major surgery, and the kind of hormones that give little girls facial hair.

My father's words echoed in my elephantine ears: *"You should have been born a boy. You should have . . ."* It was a constant refrain, along with "What good are you? You're nothing but a two-bit punk." That one I first heard after I wouldn't be coerced into granting him sexual favors. I guess if I wasn't going to put out, all he could do was act out. He filled my ears with so much shit that my innocence pretty much went out the window. Shutting out his words and pushing away his hands made my childhood one long string of heart-racing days and frightening nights. The one thread that got me through was learning to embrace my fear, to realize that terror, above all else, is a great motivator. I began to fight like a tigress: before I had nails, I had claws.

And the jungle didn't get any safer as I got older. Men kept jumping out of the bushes, giving me testosterone-fueled kicks to the solar plexus.

Take Sly Stallone. (What? You thought you'd have to wait a while before we got back to the name-dropping part? Please. I'm Janice, the world's first supermodel, and like Scheherazade I have stories to spare.)

Think of the following as a little primer of things to come in this book.

On the topic of Sly, let me tell you, when it comes to opening lines, I've gotta hand it to Romeo Rocky. The first thing he said to me after he got a load of my slim little thirtysomething body was: "Yo, Janice—looks to me like you've got to get to a gym."

A *gym! Me?!* "Hey, Sly," I said, "I was on the cover of *Vogue* before you learned to spell *Rambo.*" I mean, who was this guy to go dissing me while he's standing there in his custom-made elevator shoes? I don't *think* so.

But I let Sly take me to the gym, where he showed me how to use those gigantic, glistening, silver weight machines, which were supposedly there to "enhance my muscle groups." "Can I have some steroids?" I wondered aloud, but Sly just gave me his best steely, hangdog look, with a dash of standard Italian macho attitude. In other words, *My way or the highway, little girl.* (Years later, I smiled when I heard he had two daughters with wife Jennifer Flavin. I bet the minute his new baby daughters took their first wavering little steps, he made them log an hour apiece on the treadmill. Feel the burn, *then* feed the formula.)

When I was his babe, back in the day, Sly treated me well—well, sort of. One day, Mr. Famous stuffed four hundred bucks smack in the palm of my well-manicured hand. Frankly, I wasn't that impressed; four C-notes wouldn't even get me a decent Dolce and Gabbana skirt. When I found out why he was offering the cash, though, I was actually *pissed*. "This is for a gym membership," he grumbled in that way he has, like he's sucking on a bag of marbles while talking.

Of course, I took the money and spent it on a pair of fabulous Dior fishnet stockings to go with my new Manolo Blahniks. "You'll never make it in Hollywood," Sly reminded me as I rolled on my fishnets. "You're not perfect enough." To shut him up, I pulled out the old Visa card and charged a few months at the gym, all the while muttering, "Why, oh, why is dating always so damn *expensive?*"

While we were a couple, Sly even found a way to incorporate his three passions: himself, me, and sweat—and I'm not talking about morning quickies. When I joined him in balmy Florida on the set of his dud movie *The Specialist*, he practically shoved me out of a warm bed at five-thirty in the morning.

Instead of using this time for something sane—like having room service bring a tray of Bloody Marys and mushroom egg-white omelets up to the balcony of our luxury hotel suite—Mr. $20-Million-per-Movie had me follow him to a local high school football field. As the sun peeked out for the first time of the day, Sly would stand there in the dewy, moldy grass and yell, "Janice, we're going to do lunges." (Of course, this wasn't entirely foreign territory for me: I'd done plenty of lunging beating the other bitches to the best pumps at the Jimmy Choo annual sale.)

"Working it hard is how an actor prepares," Sly said. My mind was on overload at this point. Stay with me: *He* was acting in this movie; *I* was just there to hang out. Question: What was I preparing for, Sly?

I never expected an answer from the man who turned "yo" into an acceptable international greeting. Later on, I figured it out for myself. I was getting ready for what we're all supposed to do in this life as women: I was prepping to embody perfection for my man. What a relief when I finally discovered what a crock *that* is.

———————

The best advice I ever got had nothing to do with facial scrubs or moisturizers. It was more a cleanser for the soul.

My good friend John Lennon put it all in perspective for me.

One morning, at the height of my supermodelhood, I was leaving my New York apartment to go to the drugstore and there was John Lennon walking down the street. Imagine! I glanced his way and locked eyes with someone who looked serene, happy, and at peace with the universe. Suddenly this Lone Ranger strolled up to me, but he wasn't dressed in white: this Beatle was wearing a hot pink beret, jeans, and a yellow polka dot shirt. I've always had an affinity for rock royalty, but this was just too much. I would have fallen to my knees and wept, if it wouldn't have ruined a good pair of Gaultier jeans.

"What's wrong, luv?" John said, taking another step toward me. "You look so sad."

He asked for it. "I just feel so ugly. I have my period so I need to buy some Midol. Then I have to meet my boyfriend, who I don't even want to see because I feel so hideous," I replied, waiting for him to run for the hills.

Instead, Lennon just looked into my eyes. He was *listening to me.* I couldn't believe it. The least I could do was make him smile. "As miserable as I am," I said, "I do like your hat."

In the most gallant manner, he took the beret off and placed it on my head. (I still treasure it to this day.) "Don't be miserable, luv," he said, tossing some of his serenity in my direction. "You're the loveliest thing alive." Then he broke into a little dance right there on the sidewalk and started to sing: "*Whenever I feel afraid, I whistle a happy tune . . .*" And he actually began to *whistle,* working his soft-shoe number right there on the desolate New York concrete.

My eyes welled up with tears, but suddenly I was feeling quite lovely inside.

John even came with me to the pharmacy and talked to me while I bought my Midol. On the way out he said, "If your date doesn't work out, why don't we just have a picnic in the park?"

As of that moment, my date wasn't working out.

I waited patiently (Yoko, don't hate me) while John ran upstairs to his apartment to grab some cheese and wine. Sitting on a torn wool blanket on a crystal-clear spring day in Central Park, John said the words that made me want to change my life—and, when I thought of them again years later, write this book.

"You don't have to live up to anyone's expectations, luv," he said. "They should live up to yours. You don't have to impress anyone—they have to impress *you*."

It was a perfect moment. For every Rolling Stone who gathered no moss when it came to women, I now see there's also a Beatle to get under your skin. Mick Jagger, eat your heart out.

PART I
MODELING

I was staying at the most expensive hotel in the Bahamas on a trip for *Vogue* recently when I spied a woman across the pool. She was having a fight to the death with this very baggy, very hot (in a good way) designer bathing suit, and the damned Lycra cost-a-month's-rent suit wasn't cooperating. Naturally, our heroine did the obvious thing: she cursed, smoked, drank real Coke, and looked like she was going to have a nervous breakdown in the midday sun.

Seeing that she could use a few words of wisdom from this Big Dog, I put on my beige Manolo Blahnik stiletto pool sandals and sauntered over to her in the sexiest way. (How, exactly? We'll talk later.)

"Honey," I said, approaching her as she shot me the look of death. I didn't blame her: there are times in life when the last thing you need is some tall model getting in your face with swimsuit advice. But I felt it was my duty, as a fellow member of the X chromosome set, to go on.

"*Hello?* I can feel your pain," I whispered while she continued to adjust and glare. "I had to wear that exact suit when I was shot by Irwin Penn for *Vogue*. It took me and three stylists five hours to get me into that

fucking suit, and it only fit right because, a few months before, I got myself a brand new pair of 36C's to hold it up."

The woman stopped her tugging and stared up at me. *Now* she was interested.

"On top of that, I spent two hours in hair and makeup. Then three assistants had to use large workman's clamps to get my surgically enhanced body into that suit, but it still didn't fit right. Finally someone had to open a seam on the suit and sew me into it. Oh, and later they retouched the photos in the computer," I said. Then, for good measure: "I'm only telling you this because maybe you saw the suit in the magazine with me in it. Maybe you thought, 'Hot suit. I don't care how much it costs. I want to look like that.' Well, I'm here to tell you it's impossible for you or me to ever look like that without a team of beauty experts riding shotgun."

By that point the woman—a very pretty blonde in her late twenties with an almost perfect bod—put out her cigarette, grabbed a Kleenex, and almost burst into tears.

"I thought it was me," she sobbed. "I kept thinking, 'What's wrong with me? After spending six hundred dollars on a bathing suit, I still can't make it look right!' I figured my body was just falling apart."

"I had to pose in that suit for five hours," I told her. "By the time we were done I was ready to go under the knife again myself—who *wouldn't*

Sir Albert Watson—the one and only.

want to make that suit look the way some moronic designer intended? Thing is—it's literally impossible.

"But I tried," I told her. "And so can you."

"Have you got any of those workman's clamps in your bag?"

As the first of my kind, I think it's my duty to tell you there is absolutely no way you can look like a fucking supermodel in real life—unless your real life comes equipped with a stylist, a hair and makeup team, a clothing allowance, perfect lighting, and zero humidity. You must also move to a climate where it never rains, so your flat-ironed hair won't bend like it's giving you the finger. There. It had to be said.

Stop torturing yourself by spending hours in the john with straight irons, hundreds of dollars on fashions that don't make sense, and countless miserable moments thinking, *"Why wasn't I born looking like Cindy Crawford?"* Cindy Crawford wasn't born looking like Cindy Crawford. A highly paid team put her together and turned her into Cindy, and you can't hire them: she's got them booked for the next three decades. (Radu, call me! I love you! I have all your tapes!)

Even we supermodels can't always afford to have that team of pros living out in the garage seven days a week, following us around until the wee hours of the morning or whenever else we need them. Trust me, I wish I could: I go out to run errands about six times a day, and in Beverly Hills you never know who you'll run into while you're out stocking up on carbs for your kids.

If you're sitting around wondering how you can look like Stephanie Seymour's left thigh, quit starving yourself for a minute and listen up. Janice is going to tell you a few stories about how models get to look so fabulous. I'm talking pain, drugs, barfing, and near-death experiences. Sure, occasionally it's a great gig. Sometimes you get to keep the clothes. Sometimes you steal them. But I'll save that story for later.

The more I look back on my many adventures as Supermodel 1.0, the more I come back around to my favorite disclaimer: models aren't stupid—not all of us, anyway. I've said it before: most of us can walk and talk and drink champagne from a slipper, all at the same time. Some of us even ask ourselves big questions, like: *Why do Dior sunglasses cost so much? Does Calista Flockhart have hips? Shouldn't Valentino run for president with Donna Karan as his running mate?*

Then of course there's my personal favorite: *What the hell does it all mean?* Come follow the Big Dog as we scrounge our way through the modeling world to sniff out the answers.

1.

Going All the Way for Perfection

How far will your average supermodel go to look fabulous before, during, and after the hot-hot days of a modeling career? Well, let's take a quick trek down Memory Lane to Perfection Junction because highlights like this—well, they ain't pretty.

The Origins of Perfection

At age fourteen, naturally, I was no supermodel—not just yet. But I *wanted* to be one, so badly that I practically slept with *Vogue* under my pillow. I guess I was hoping some beauty tips would invade my brain while I slept. Instead, I ended up with my first pair of fake boobs.

When I say I stuffed myself every day, I don't mean gorging on burgers and fries. I filled my training bra to the brim (or as far as those baby cups could go) with tons of good old-fashioned affordable Kleenex.

Now, remember, I grew up in Florida. That means 100-degree temps and 200 percent humidity—so let's just say it wasn't exactly comfortable when all those tissues started getting moist and sticky. But I *needed* bigger boobs, and there was no way I was waiting around for Mother Nature's blessing—much less for Victoria to reveal her secrets to me. At fourteen I couldn't really afford implants, so I did the next best thing and started reaching out to bathroom products. I never thought of it in my virginal state, but my slogan should have been *Please don't squeeze the Charmin*.

One night I took my toilet-paper-packing self to the high school basketball game. I remember feeling a little strange midway through the second half, a little . . . lighter. *Maybe skipping lunch is working!* I thought.

Then, in a moment of horror, I looked down into the bleachers and saw a soggy, sweaty, melting ball of toilet paper on the floor below me. One of my counterfeit boobs had staged its own escape by leaping out of my bra and T-shirt. When I stood up to cheer the team on, I had one big tit and one nonexistent one, and there wasn't much I could do about it. In a million years I couldn't have endured that long, humiliating walk down the bleachers to hit the bathroom and wad myself up again.

Ever the clever girl, I thought of the next best thing to rectify the situation. When no one was looking, I carefully slipped off a Ped sock and, while everyone else was cheering for the Nova Titans, granted myself a new second boob. I was like the Bionic Woman: *We can rebuild her!* A few minutes later my clammy hands were raised in fists to cheer—and my fake tits (both of them) were bouncing along for the ride.

That night, when my mother asked what I wanted for my next birthday, I surprised her. "Ten new pairs of Peds," I said. "But without the little pom-poms." No one had nipples that big.

Oh, the Horror

Okay, enough about my youth (for now, anyway). Let's pick things up in the backseat of a limo, circa 1980, after a *Harper's Bazaar* shoot for

Gucci. I was making out with rocker Frank Zappa before we stepped out for dinner at the fabulous Russian Tea Room in New York City.

As the two of us strutted inside the place, all eyes were on my hot white jeans, which left little to the imagination. Somewhere between the antipasto and the second bottle of vino, I looked down and noticed something clammy between my legs—something that had nothing to do with Frank. Perfect, hot, model-babe Janice had all of a sudden turned into just-got-her-period-all-over-her-Calvins Janice.

What to do?

Before Frank got a load of the problem and decided I needed a transfusion (yep, it was that bad), my brain went into overdrive. Suddenly my hand was spilling half a bottle of wine into my nether regions.

"Oh my God, Frank, you had me so hot I wasn't paying attention," I purred as $200 worth of booze soaked into my crotch. I could always get hold of another bottle of wine—but at least this way I knew I wouldn't end up as the bleeding girl on one of his anthology albums!

Out of Africa, Into a Mess

I went to Africa once on a shoot for *Playboy*, and my body was crying out for a hunky native. Since the only one in sight had what looked like a large bone through his nostrils, I opted to focus on myself and my other need: relief for my dehydrated body. Hearing my cries for some spa activity, my handlers suggested I go roll around in a mud bath. All I could think was, *Why not?* Sounded like a cheaper, more rustic version of the $300 mud wrap they offer at any Ritz Carlton.

Well, it was a tad more Farmer in the Dell than I expected. In fact, it was a giant mud pit. Sure, it was sort of interesting to feel that cold, smooth clay go into places previously reserved for men I invited into my bedroom. The downside was, I couldn't get the mud out of those private spots, no matter how high I reached or how hard I tried.

Eventually I found myself in photographer Peter Beard's tub, which was actually a rusty tin can in the middle of this hog ranch where we were shooting. On the plus side, though, Peter's servants *did* bring pots brimming with hot, steamy water to get the mud out of . . . well, I'll leave that to your imagination. At least I could finally claim I was *earthy*.

The Mile-High Club Revisited

We've all heard of the mile-high club, but this is actually a *clean* story (literally) about me getting naked on a plane. In 1982, I had a hot date with a zillionaire whose name I can't even mention, or he'll send his henchmen. I *can* tell you that I was flying to this playboy's mansion, but certainly not squeezed into some middle seat on United or Delta. Please. My boyfriend-to-be sent his friend Mohammad Khashoggi's private jet.

At thirty-eight thousand feet I was happily sipping champagne when I realized I'd developed that ol' airplane stench—your skin gets that glossy look, your pits start to smell, and you feel like your entire body has just been dipped in a vat of grease. *What to do?* No prob. The plane had a full bathroom with a shower and I, Janice, knew I'd better make the most of it. My date was picking me up at the airport, so I had to look hot, not feel like I'd been working a vat of fries at Burger King.

"But, Miss," said our friendly but annoying steward, "we're flying through a thunderstorm, and I must have you buckled up. You are not allowed to stand. FAA regulations." I raised one perfectly plucked brow and said, "Look, honey, if we go down, I'm not going to have flat hair and BO. I'll smell good and I'll be wearing Chanel lipstick. I'm getting up, so get the shower ready."

A few minutes later, as the plane dropped five thousand feet and we temporarily lost cabin pressure, I was grasping a bar of Bulgari soap and cursing while trying to shave my legs. Ever tried to moisturize in a plane that's swaying sideways? Don't even get me started. Even the good products don't work in extreme conditions, and I don't know what's more extreme than naked turbulence at cruising altitude. The friendly fucking skies! What a myth.

Having Her Cake

Beverly Johnson and I were in the Bahamas once, sitting by the pool deck, when I did the unfathomable: I ordered us *an entire chocolate cake* the day before the shoot. You can picture the look on the face of our waiter: I'm sure he thought the cake should come with a complimentary airport puke bag. Models might pop *out of* cakes, but if the frosting even hit their lips, it would be upchuck time, right?

"Miss, you just want one teeny piece of cake?" the waiter offered, like some kind of Caribbean Richard Simmons trying to keep me in line.

"No—what part of this don't you understand?" I said. "I want the entire cake—and two forks. Oh, and two Diet Cokes." (Ladies, am I right? You can eat a million calories, but stick with *Diet* Coke and you'll be okay.)

Eventually Waiter Boy delivered my death by chocolate in its entirety, and I dove in like I'd just come home from a desert island. Beverly just sat there staring at me, her eyes bugging out of her head, but I couldn't stop shoveling the cake into my face. (For the record, she ate a few bites, too.) I just kept inhaling chocolate buttercream—even though all the while I knew that in ten hours I'd be slipping on a skin-tight, mole-showing Karl Lagerfeld evening gown. At one point I wiped some frosting off my upper lip and said a silent prayer to the spirit of flat stomachs. Then I promptly went to the bathroom and puked my guts out.

Believe me, I'm not making light of anorexia or bulimia here, but it happened. I gave up hiding things a long time ago (with my *last* book).

Fortunately, I was born practically emaciated and stayed that way my entire life. But I knew I had a problem that day in the Bahamas because I was using the cake to fill me up, and I needed to lose it so I could properly and perfectly fill out a gown. What was really messed up was that I knew I didn't *need* to barf because any photographer could just lop off ten pounds, or an afternoon of deviant cake behavior, with a little judicious Photoshop. Actually, it kills me to know how many young girls beat themselves up trying to look like the models in the magazines today, when at this point it's just technically *impossible*: you can't make human flesh behave like an artist's perfectly arranged pixels.

Still, I'm comforted to realize that it's a two-way street: average girls might not look like the models they see in magazines—but, as the cake story suggests, neither do models like Janice. The boys with the magic digital wands will fix it later.

The Flip Side

Of course, I've also been known to starve myself, which means not eating *at all* for two or three days before a shoot. That's why I passed out in the Rome airport after an important Valentino shoot. Unfortunately, Howard Fugel, my hair and makeup guy, had my wallet, my passport, and my cash with him for safekeeping, and the moron got on the plane, and let it take off, without noticing that my face was plastered to the cold and dirty tile floor in the airport waiting area.

So when I woke up, I was faced with a pretty sucky situation: $11.30 in my pocket, in a foreign country with no passport, and some weird Roman floor grime all over my face. (Exfoliant—*stat!*) I had to take a cab back to Valentino headquarters, where I waited for a few days until I could track Howard down and get him to FedEx my stuff back. Until then, all I could think of was my warm bed and all the beauty products lined up on my all-American bathroom counter.

Who says modeling is such a perfect job?

The Perfect Pout

Here's a story that bites. I was shooting a cover for *Cosmo*, getting ready to let loose with my biggest smile, when suddenly the temporary cap on my front tooth decided to leap off its post and hibernate for winter under my tongue. What was left in its place was one cracked tooth—and the stomach pains I was getting from anxiety over having to tell the photographer, who I was sure would replace me on the spot.

As if God was watching out for me, five seconds into my tooth trauma the photographer had to readjust the lighting, and I was shipped off for a hair and makeup touchup. "I'll do my own lipstick," I insisted, ignoring the curious look from the makeup chick, who must have assumed I was just being bitchy. As I lathered on the Estee Lauder, I sat there scheming furiously, desperate to come up with a plan.

Back in front of the camera, I got my inspiration. Before I had a chance to open my mouth, I dropped my usual smile and went with my best pout instead—a pout embedded in my otherwise petrified face. Suddenly, the whole room—designers, photographers, stylists, editors, assistants, even the caterers—were absorbed in watching my every move.

"Oh my God, what smoldering sexuality!" said a designer.

"Look at all that attitude!" said an editor.

"She's an inspiration to women everywhere who just want to tell the world to *fuck off*," said a catering guy.

I just kept quiet and churned out the smolder, trying to keep my tongue away from my jagged tooth while thinking up ways to kill my dentist. I might have felt like the Jed Clampett of the modeling world, but I took the pain and turned it into attitude-a-gogo.

Boiling It Down

Just before a major bathing suit shoot for Richard Avedon, I had a boil on my leg burst. The pain was so intense that I wanted to crumble in a heap on the floor, but once again the look on my face said *hot, sexy, cool.*

"I want you to look like you're tormented, Janice," Avedon told me.

"No problem," I said, wincing.

The next day, I checked myself into a hospital.

"Miss, you might have blood poisoning," the doc said.

"Does blood poisoning scar?" I asked.

He just rolled his eyes.

Hand Job

This is a good one: When my idea of becoming the world's first super-model was still in its embryonic stage (in other words, when I was broke, struggling, and living in a roach-infested apartment in New York), I read about an open call for Revlon models. After walking about five miles to the audition because I couldn't afford bus fare, I still arrived a little early. So I popped into the nearest Duane Reade drugstore and started brows-ing around until my eyes went *"boiiing"* — I knew at once I'd spotted the thing that would put me on the map.

In my quest for perfection, I spent two days' food money on a box of ultrared henna. Then I snuck into the drugstore bathroom and pumped up the volume of my boring brunette hair right there on the spot, while some rather large woman was changing her two-year-old on the counter next to me.

Only one problem: I forgot to use gloves. As I walked out of Duane Reade, I looked down and caught myself red-handed: fingertip to wrist. My hands were stained the color of the Union 76 gas station ball. Was I horrified? That's putting it mildly. This stuff was worse than the Mystic Tan I used in the middle of January to get "a little color."

I walked into the audition looking like I just got back from some tribal ritual in Botswana. (Then again, I did get the job: my hair looked pretty good, and turned out the photographer had a jones for redheads.) A month later, when I still looked like I had the hands of a burn victim, I had to wonder if it was worth it.

Café Oh No

Another year, another horror: When I was twenty-seven, long before it be-came fashionable, my sister Debbie and I spent a summer in Southamp-ton, Long Island. Besides baking on the beach and looking for hot guys, we logged time with a fabulous nutritionist named Oz Garcia.

Deb and I were always moaning to Oz that we were much too fat, and

I really must have driven him crazy because I had a big bathing suit shoot coming up at the end of the summer. Oz told us about all sorts of Chinese herbs and drops, not to mention sending me to an acupuncturist who poked and prodded me more than any of my teenage dates. But it wasn't enough—it was never, ever enough. I was so convinced I was a fat pig that I practically overdosed on those herbs and oils.

Then, as if my metabolism weren't revved up enough, I took things one step too far. I bought a cappuccino machine, but not just to save trips to the local café for hot foam. No, I used that sucker to crank out methamphetamine lattes for myself and anyone else who wanted to saddle up and get a good jolt of Janice's "coffee plus"! Imagine showing up at Starbucks: "Hi, Janice! I'll take a Grande Druggie Metabolism Booster Double Cap with two packets of Equal." All I know is, at my coffee-plus bar no one asked for a pastry on the side.

As for me, by the time I'd slammed down one of those, my body was pulsating 24-7—to the point where I couldn't even walk anymore. I ran to the beach, ran to the shower to wash the sand out of my bikini bottom, and ran into bed to work it off with the cute, young local beach boy. (What a calorie burner!) I practically killed the kid with my extra "caffeine kick."

One crazy hot morning in August, though, I woke up and noticed that every single part of my body itched—so badly I wanted to run over every inch of my skin till it calmed down. The diagnosis? A full-body breakout of hives—bad news for a girl with a Cole of California bathing suit shoot in a few days that was going to pay her rent for the rest of the year. I got antibiotics from a local doc, but they didn't help, and I spent the rest of the summer looking like a very thin leper.

But, oh, my enablers: the photographer took one look at me and said, "Hot body, Janice—and don't worry, we'll airbrush out the hives."

Foot Job

In the interest of walking tall in my Manolos, I had an operation in the late 1980s known as a *bunectomy*. In laywoman's terms, that means the doctor hacks a big bunion off your foot. As much as I love high heels, I had suffered the worst pain of my entire life whenever I wore them. Going under the knife was my only escape.

After the operation, I was so stoned from the painkillers that somehow in my haze Dr. Janice managed to take off the bandages to check out the healing process. Then I flew to St. Barts in tears, with my foot infected, wearing the ugliest bandage ever. I asked myself: "How in the world could I wear my Tod's flats in this condition?" Mummified foot in tow, I spent a few days cursing the person (who am I kidding—the *man!*) who invented spiked footwear. The spiked punch they served at the bar did make me feel much better, if only temporarily. Was the operation worth it? Yes and no. Right now, as I write this, I'm staring at my new black Manolo summer sandals, with such a high heel I might need a stepladder to get into them—and I know I'll need another operation to fix the slipped discs in my back if I fall.

My motto: As long as the buns of my ass look good, I'm not going to worry about the ones on my feet.

Hair Now, Gone Tomorrow

We'll finish this overview of perfection pit stops with a hairy story. I can't stress enough that we should all make it our job to find, study, and memorize a picture of the late, great Diana Vreeland, former fashion editor of *Harper's Bazaar* and editor-in-chief of *Vogue*. There was a woman who knew enough not to mess with a good thing. Diana rocked the same bob hairdo her entire life for one simple reason: it was the bomb. She also knew that following trends, or trying to ape the latest movie-star do, is a great big *don't* if you've already discovered what's perfect for you.

It took me *way* too long to learn the same lesson—the hard way. In my twenties I decided to visit the fabulous hairstylist Harry King, who took one look at my luxurious brown locks and ran his hand through my celebrated mop like it was one of the wonders of the earth.

So you can imagine how I nearly put poor Harry into cardiac arrest when I told him: "Cut it all off!"

"*All* of it, darling?" said Harry, mortified. "Do you want to talk to a therapist first?"

"Completely off!" I said with bravado—and this was way before Linda Evangelista went short. I was the test case, and Harry was worried that he was going to flunk. An hour later, flipping back my liberating new do, I waltzed out of his studio and never looked back at the ten pounds of signature Janice hair on the floor.

If you did your homework from my last book, kids, you'll remember that around this time I was working on a demo record and prepping for my big singing debut at Studio 54. I was basically going for that rock-star-cool androgynous thing, which I always thought was pretty dope. Unfortunately, when I looked in the mirror for the first time, I wanted to cry out: suddenly the tight little shock of hair that framed my face looked very short—and very ugly. Fuck! I couldn't even be the perfect grungy rock star.

One day Mick stopped by the recording studio where I was working on my demo—and saw my new look.

In response, he gave me a look of his own. I think they call it "shock and horror."

"Oh my God, Janice, what did you do to your haaaaaiiiiiiirrrrr?" He put so many syllables in *hair* I thought it was the chorus of a new song.

"I'm a trendsetter, Mick."

"You don't have to cut your haaaaaaiiiiiiirrrrr to cut a record," he moaned.

I just gave him my best disgusted-model look and told the biggest rock star on the planet: "Hey! Mick! Get out of my *haaaaaaiiiirrrrr!*"

2.

Starving for Beauty

There are certain things in life so startling that your mind actually blocks them out to protect you from the shock of it all. That's why I'm amazed I have any recall when it comes to the most frightening thing I've ever witnessed in my entire life: watching made-for-TV-movie star Nicolette Sheridan scarfing down pizza at Mulberry Street Pizzeria in Beverly Hills.

Take a moment to digest that little vision yourself. If you're anything like me, your own mind might have a hard time keeping it down.

It was horrifying. I mean, here was one of the most perfect bodies alive—a resident of *Knots Landing*, no less. There were only three reasons she would carbo-load with such abandon. I had to ask myself: Had the world spun off its axis? Was this an optical illusion? Did someone create no-fat, no-calorie pizza when I wasn't looking?

I needed answers!

That's when I turned my detective's eye on Nicolette, sitting at a table with her thin actress-wannabe friends, who paled in her presence—and I'm not just talking about their hair color. Blonde, tanned, and toned,

Nic was the sexiest, most perfect thing alive, and she held court without a stitch of makeup! She had her flaxen hair carelessly tossed in two cute little pigtails; I imagined her taking thirty seconds to pop 'em in before she ran out the door of what was probably the cutest house in all of California. She was blessed by the Goddess of Good Genes and Impeccable Taste, and I hated her and loved her all at once.

But her eating habits left a lot to be desired.

"Miss, do you plan on ordering?" the bossy waitress asked me, noticing that I was drooling over Nicolette instead of the menu. She may have wondered whether I was nursing some sort of lesbian-model crush, but honestly, it wasn't that at all. I was just lusting after her lunch order.

"I'll have the house salad, no dressing, no croutons, no cheese, no avocado, no anything except lettuce, and not too much of that, either," I ordered. "Oh, and flat water."

Just saying the words, I felt so damn deprived. It was like I was plopped in the middle of the desert with nothing to sustain myself except my cute khaki outfit with matching Mac eye shadow. Meanwhile Nicolette was

Sly and Arnold's trainer George Pipisik lecturing me on diet, diet, diet.

in paradise two tables over, eating grapes off the vine and turning water into wine.

"Bread?" the waitress asked.

"Are you kidding?" I answered, but my eyes weren't on her.

They were zeroed in on my subject, Nicolette, who was now *eating* the piece of pizza. Closing my eyes, I tried to imagine the taste of real, melting cheese and chewy, spicy meats spotted with fabulous flecks of lard. Maybe it was all my modeling years catching up with me; maybe it was the fact that I'd been dieting since age eight. I just couldn't get my mind to go there. In that moment, I was convinced that just thinking the words "extra toppings" might put me over my calorie count for the decade. I had only one consolation: surely this one slice of pizza would be the only thing the poor kid ate all day.

After polishing off her slice and licking her fingers (in the most delightful way, though), Nicolette reached across the table and did something that caused my blood to chill.

She reached for another piece!

I was *fascinated*. I dropped my fork, stared even harder, and saw that her pizza wasn't even plain cheese. There was *sausage*, and . . . no, no— yes! Little red discs of pepperoni! Like a stalker intent on memorizing every move of her prey, I watched Nic chew every bite. Eventually she did something that could have gotten her disbarred from the modeling profession permanently (or at least until the stars of the WB eventually took over the print-ad world): she ate the whole pie.

Later that day, a friend of mine offered me a blueberry muffin. Knowing I had a *Vogue* shoot later that week, I plucked one blueberry off the top and said, "Mmmm—great muffin."

My rumbling stomach protested loudly as I walked away, but I just took another sip of flat water and damned the hunger pains. And I threw in a curse on the lovely Nicolette for good measure—a traitor to her kind.

I know, you're thinking, "Janice, how far did you go to be thin?" The answer is simple, my friends: pretty damn far.

I basically swore off food for the better part of two decades. That left me really, really hungry all the time. I chose to starve myself in my quest for perfection. What made it even worse was that I was a workout maniac: I would run, walk, ride bikes, do aerobics, high-intensity step, and yoga—sometimes all in one day. I did Radu before Radu was Radu.

Let me throw it all out there: Yep, I did toss my cookies to get even thinner. (Not that I ever *ate* cookies, but you get the idea.) I went bulimic during a Bahamas shoot for some fancy perfume whose name I couldn't even pronounce. My nose was otherwise occupied, anyway. I did so much coke that I spent half the shoot throwing up. It should go without saying that I don't condone this as a weight-loss plan, either. That was a terrible time for my body. I threw up and then starved myself for days, all the time convinced that I'd stumbled on the perfect "lifestyle and body maintenance plan."

When I *was* eating (not an everyday occurrence), I tried the grapefruit diet, the pasta diet, and the cabbage soup diet (not so good if you plan to be in a room with anyone else who has working nostrils, we're talking *eau du hell*). I also found the anorexic just-don't-eat-anything diet to be a simple way to keep the pounds off.

My best diet back then was the bread diet. I know you're not supposed to eat bread now, but on my plan, today's carb theories didn't really matter. I just ate one piece of dry toast, *period*. That was it for the entire day. And if that went down the hatch in the morning, by dusk I was pretty weak and shaky—although my Calvins slipped on with ease. That pretty much sums up the 1970s for me.

During the 1980s, I was on the "pick, pick, pick model's plan." That's where you never really order yourself a meal, you just sit yourself down next to a friend who's willing to order an actual meal for himself (never *her*self—the other models never ordered meals, either), then pick a few bites off that person's plate and call it a day. During those years, I never ate much at all. To me, a bite of steak, two green beans, one bite of a roll, and a grape were about all I'd allow myself in a twenty-four-hour period. I just picked my way toward staying thin.

What choice did I have? You've got to be less than 0, sizewise, to fit into those plus-priced designer clothes. I honestly believe that Valentino designs his clothes to begin at a size I would call negative 12. Models know the drill when it comes to fitting into these outfits: you just ignore your aching stomach and drink water to kill the hunger pains. That works to your advantage because all that water makes you lose even more weight. In my mind, I would pretend the water was a delicious strawberry milkshake; some days I was creative enough to convince myself it was a triple-fudge Blizzard from Dairy Queen.

If you think about it hard enough, you can almost convince yourself. *Almost.*

But it isn't just models who are on this kind of plan. There are plenty of regular women, and even plenty of men, who want to look like models and don't care how much it hurts to get there.

I understand all that. I don't like it, but I understand it.

Back in the day, though, I looked for every reason I could find to believe I was on the right track. And in the 1980s I managed to get my dieting follies sanctioned by none other than the leader of the free world: President Ronald Reagan.

The occasion was a presidential fund-raising dinner at the fabulous Le Cirque restaurant in New York City. Just the thought of gazing at the man with the keys to the Oval Office made my heart flutter—and I don't even think it was the amphetamines.

I'm no Monica, but all that power sure makes me purr. If I were the First Lady, I can't help thinking, things would be a little different in the Oval Office. I'd be the first First Lady with a slit up her Azzedine Alaia femme fatale skirt.

But I digress. I was so nervous about the whole idea of dining with the First Fam, I spent the two days before the dinner feasting on diet pills, coke, uppers, downers, and just about everything else I could get my hands on. You could say I had taken a pharmacy the night before. I was flying on narcotics and nerves—a pretty scary mix.

My dates for the evening were the two owners of Zenon, a hot-hot-hot New York disco that was giving Studio 54 a little competition. Giannina Faccio (now Mrs. Ridley Scott) tagged along; we were one happy, bone-thin, stomach-rumbling, chic table. The only thing I couldn't wrap my mind around was the idea that I was attending a *dinner*. Was eating actually required? Who knew?

No matter: I had no appetite anyway. I could hardly chew what was a perfectly lovely roast beef, accompanied by an evil-looking blob of mashed potatoes and a boring little stack of green beans. Honestly, I wouldn't have known how to eat this dinner if I'd tried: I'd given up red meat sometime around the sixth grade. Instead of eating, I just drank in the other celebrities while downing my fourth glass of champagne. In one corner was a preening Andy Warhol; in another I spotted a drop-dead-gorgeous Bianca Jagger in a sheer red cocktail dress; seeing her was all the sustenance I needed.

"Janice, you know, you should try to eat something," said one of my dinner companions. "You're expected to at least chew every few minutes." I plucked exactly one almond sliver off my green beans, bit off half of it, and retorted, "Are you satisfied? I am. In fact, I'm stuffed."

How could he expect me to digest when the diet pills had me so hyped up? I'd been downing those pills like they were chalky little Valentine hearts. Why? So I could be superskinny enough to attend fabulous dinner parties and eat absolutely nothing.

Suddenly I looked up—and the First Lady of the United States of America was hovering over me, looking like someone's extremely well-dressed mother.

"Hello, my dear," said Nancy Reagan, who obviously didn't notice the fact that I was about to pass out from a one-two punch of nerves and low blood sugar. This tiny woman—who slept every night with the head honcho of the United States—then hit me up for a little advice. "I must ask you a quick question, dear. How do you stay so thin?"

Now, it wasn't like Mrs. R was pushing a size 26 or anything. She was such a bag of skinny bones that I saw her actual skeleton protruding through her pink Chanel evening suit. Those two "C's" guarded her breasts like a high-fashion bulletproof vest.

Glancing sideways, I could see that her husband, our fearless leader, had no such problem with weight. He certainly didn't worry about eating too much, either. The evidence: two slices of thick roast beef between his lips, and about a quarter-cup of grease dripping out of his mouth. You'd think one of the Secret Service guys could hand the Prez a napkin.

"Mrs. Reagan," I stammered sweetly, swallowing my fear. "Forget about me being thin. What's with Ronnie and that big, greasy roast beef dinner?"

Inside I wondered if you could get locked up for mocking the President's table manners. I knew I'd never make it through prison alive; all the top stylists told me gray wasn't my color, and I knew a boiled wool prison uniform would tear up my waxed bod. (Not to mention that I like to pick and choose my lesbian encounters, not have them thrust upon me by some hulking Bertha doing 20 to life.)

Lucky for me, the First Lady just laughed warmly at my social slip. And she perked up even more when I changed the subject to one of her favorites—astrology.

"You know, I'm an Aquarius," I chirped. "Abe Lincoln was an Aquarius! And Ron—your husband and my fabulous, smart, and handsome President—is an Aquarius. So what are the odds on me getting his autograph?"

I guess my upfront approach was working. No one was standing over me with handcuffs.

Mrs. R smiled broadly, touched my slightly quivering shoulder, and said, "Janice, you're exactly what Ronnie needs right now. Come with me, dear."

Who was I to argue with the First Lady? It wasn't like I was missing out on the meal I wasn't eating, so I stood and sashayed toward the most powerful man in the world.

On the walk over to the President, I kept mentioning fellow Aquarians to her. "Did you know Bob Dylan is one?" I asked Nancy, who seemed charmed enough to motion the Secret Service away with just the crook of one of her jeweled fingers. I was *in love* with this woman. What power! What diamonds!

And then I was on.

Standing in front of the President of the United States, I smiled and then did the only thing I could think of to calm everyone's nerves: I jumped right into his lap. Two Secret Service guys finally woke up and stepped forward, but President Reagan just took my arm lightly, shucking those big gun-toting dudes off with his other hand.

Two minutes ago I'd have been worried about getting grease on my dress. Suddenly, though, I didn't care; after all, it would be a historic stain. (And this in the days before presidential dress stains became a fashion statement.)

"Now, what can I do for you?" President Reagan asked, putting down his steak knife and grinning at me. I thought, *This man was an actor—he knows a few things about women jumping in his lap. What could I do for* him? Still, I tried to behave, willing myself to think the kind of patriotic and serious thoughts that would have made my high school history teacher proud. *I pledge allegiance . . . We the people . . . I'm just a bill, yes, I'm only a bill . . .* I knew that wasn't going to get me very far, though, so I launched into my main reason for my little lap visit.

"Sir, your wife said I could get your autograph," I said with all the moxie in my twenty-five-year-old body.

One of the President's friends, Jerry Zipkin, was sitting to his left. He leaned over and said, "Miss Dickinson, you were fabulous in the Calvin Klein show." *That* seemed to catch the President's attention. For a split second I started wondering if there was a cabinet position in my future: Director of Sex Appeal? Secretary of Style?

President Reagan changed the subject. "You're so thin, young lady," he said. "What do you eat?" Suddenly he sounded like the father I wished I'd had.

All I could think of was that side of beef he'd been wolfing down a minute ago.

"I don't have much of an appetite right now, sir," was all I could muster. "By the way, what should I call you: Mr. President? Ronald? Ronnie?"

"First of all, it doesn't matter if you don't eat anything because you're fabulous," he said. And with a wink he added, "Oh, and you can call me Ronnie."

I didn't eat for the next twenty-four hours. Even the most powerful man in the universe was condoning my eating habits. I'd been given a new lifetime appointment: All-Time Leader of Lean. I could tour the globe and tell our fat foreign friends: "For God's sake, for the future of the world, *put down that damn piece of bread.*"

Before we move on from weight control and modeling, though, I want to take a minute and talk about the really dark side of being thin. The fact is, there's a dirty little secret in the modeling world, at the place where weight loss meets job loss. (What? You didn't think we were smart enough to combine the two?)

Let me start from the beginning.

Models aren't exactly kind to their fellow beauties—to say the least. This is a cutthroat business, with enormous amounts of money on the line, and every so often a pretty face will go pretty far to make sure she gets the job over someone else.

Take the case of the late, great Gia Carangi. Gia, one of the top models of the late 1970s, died tragically of AIDS at the young age of twenty-six. She was the most sexual, sarcastic being who ever walked the face of this earth. Well, Gia gave my friend and fellow model Bitten Knudsen a grape one day for lunch. (I bet that's all she ate that day.) But it wasn't exactly a pure piece of fruit: Gia had marinated the grape in ipecac syrup, that pink stuff that parents use to get their children to throw up (also given to poisoning victims so they'll hurl out the bad stuff). It was the perfect sabotage tactic—Bitten spent the entire day in the john tossing her cookies, while Gia was charming two designers who'd been trying to decide which of the two stunning beauties to use for a major shoot. Guess who got the job?

Over-the-counter tricks like ipecac are well known in the modeling business because the truth of the matter is that girls have been using the stuff for years as a diet aid. For a model who just can't stick two fingers down her gullet to lose her dinner, it's much easier to take a swig of syrup and say good-bye (a very messy, disgusting good-bye) to all that steak and potatoes. I'm almost afraid to talk about all this here because I hate to think about inspiring a run on ipecac at Walgreens. All I can say is, please don't try this at home: it's not a joke, it's the start of a full-fledged eating disorder.

Gia may have used the stuff for her own purposes, but don't think she was unique in her approach. On one trip I took to Italy, I watched a group of runway models who were practically using the syrup as one of the four major food groups. Those pasta-loving *puntas* snuck into the dressing room of a group of Brazilian models they hated (*So lean! So goddam tan!*) and used that syrup to spike their Diet Cokes and spice up their salads.

Let's just say it wasn't a good day for international relations (or bathroom etiquette). Those bitchy Brazilian girls weren't idiots: they made sure that the pizza delivered to the Italian roaches had a little "something extra."

In the end, it was a great day for America: I was the only American there, and I was fasting that week—the natural way.

What's left to say about all the eating disorders I dealt with over the years? All I can cop to is that my years as a supermodel sparked my lifelong struggle to achieve a perfect size and shape for my body. Good looking was never good enough. When it came to breast implants, once wasn't enough, so I had them done again. My first pair were saline; later I had them replaced with silicone because I thought it would make me look even better. Can you imagine? I was never satisfied, never happy—never at peace—when I looked in the mirror. Sad, huh?

In the mid-1980s, I'd go to Karen Voight's exercise class in Los Angeles and stand in a sea of women who reminded me of a herd of perfumed cattle. (To the lady in front of me: you didn't really need to *bathe* in the Shalimar. That stink melted off half the lining in my nostrils.) I didn't understand what training was all about back then; I could hardly stand to hear the word. "Today, I have to train," the other models would say, and I would just cringe. I wasn't trying out for the fucking Olympics; I just wanted to fit into a size 0. When it came to the perfect waist for a pair of designer Calvins, though, I was a 10.0 type of gal.

Back when I was on a runway, I didn't even know how to work out properly. I sweated my way through these aerobic meltdowns (with no food in my stomach), expecting to drop dead on a mat at any moment and watch from above as the other cattle girls did two hops and a twist over my dead body. I knew I'd be found under the Shalimar queen, who looked equally exhausted and ready to die.

When you're a model, you can never step back and enjoy your body of work—because your work *is* your body.

The only time I calmed down for more than two seconds was during a shoot in China. I noticed that the most lovely Chinese women and men would stand in the middle of the streets every morning and do *tai chi*. Suddenly it dawned on me. I didn't need to enroll in some high-priced exercise class, taught by some stick-thin know-it-all with the annoying voice of a high school cheerleader. All I needed was to gather a little knowledge and "train" myself.

From then on, it didn't matter if I was in Washington Square Park, South Beach, or Venice Beach. All I had to do was take a morning walk, dodge the local coke dealers on the street, and scout out a nice park bench to do my dips. I used my hotel nightstand to tone my triceps, and learned to run down and up any available staircase. The solitude of working my body on my own time saved my sanity during those days—and still does.

Yes, I loved suffering for beauty. But it's so much better to suffer in private.

3.

Are All Models Lesbians?

The answer is simple: Absolutely.

Let me tell you a little story. Back in the days of Studio 54, at the height of my affair with a certain Rolling Stone, I was comforting a fellow model when I discovered that she had, um, a *soft* spot for me, too. While I was making time with Mick, this supermodel was rolling that other Stone, Mr. Ron Wood. The problem was, Ron was married to a fabulous friend of mine named Jo, while this model—a gorgeous platinum blond beauty we'll call "Pia"—was just one of my fellow models.

Ron and Pia's wild and crazy affair was taking them to all ends of the earth as he trailed along behind her from shoot to shoot.

After some time, though, Pia grew tired of sharing Ron with his wife. Just banging a rock star wasn't enough for Pia. Finally fed up with the love triangle, Pia shows up at my place one night in tears.

"Pia, it's damn cool to be tweaking a rock legend," I say. "Believe me, I know. I mean, Mick is—" *Hold it, Janice. For once, this isn't about you—thank God.* Instead I just give her a sad smile and pull my trump card. "Pia, if Ron was a plumber and not a Rolling Stone, would you really want to be with him? Would you want to be Mrs. I-Plunge-Toilets? Can you tell me you love this man so much you'd be willing to live with him in a two-bedroom walkup with shag carpeting from the seventies?"

That obviously cuts her pretty deep. Pia looks up at me and says . . . "Well, couldn't we replace the carpeting?"

"Come on, Pia, I'm taking you home," I say, grabbing her perfectly manicured fingers and ushering her into my car. Feeling pretty impressed with my newfound ability to resolve domestic disputes, I drive Pia back to her house; one thing leads to another, and before long I'm crossing the line, stepping in as her unofficial "relationship therapist."

Pia and I ended up spending an awesome evening together—having the best sex ever. Maybe it was her grief at losing one of the greatest rock guitarists in history, or maybe she was just horny. Maybe it was the faint taint of Shalimar I'd picked up from that bitch at the gym. Whatever. I wouldn't call it a lesbian affair, but as girl-on-girl interludes go, it was hot, wet, and wild.

The next morning, hung over on the world's best champagne, Pia and I were lying in her bed when suddenly Pia's maid popped in to "straighten things up." I'm not sure if that included getting me out of Pia's bed, but I immediately felt a bad vibe coming from this cleaning woman, who looked a little judgmental (not to mention jealous) as she stared at my naked breasts in the soft yellow sunlight.

As for Pia, she just pulled the covers over her head. Not one to take any bullshit, I popped my head up from the feather pillow and yelled at the maid, "Get out of here. *You're fired!*" Two girls in one room were enough; I didn't have the energy for a threesome.

My one night with Pia remains an awesome memory, and I've shared it with other models who have their own similar stories. And when I say that all models are lesbians—in some way, shape, or form—it's all the proof I need. Why not? You get to have sex, swap shoes, and that toilet seat stays *down* at all times. Sure, you might have to fight over a blow dryer now and then—but when you've got someone nearby who knows how important it is to hold your hair while you throw up, who's complaining?

4.

War Stories from the Beauty Front Lines

During my modeling career, there were moments when I thought to my-self, *You know what, Janice? Thinking is just too hard—and it's going to cre-ate fine lines.* Frankly, when you're a model, no one expects you to use too many brain cells anyway. "Janice," Calvin Klein had told me, "models aren't supposed to think." And quite often I went along with Calvin's Rule, just dropping all my worries and turning my mind off. *After all,* I thought, *I was just a dumb model, right? Who was I to go around* thinking?

Well, whenever I stopped, I got myself into some deep shit—including some pretty life-threatening situations. All in the name of my so-called "art."

Modeling is a damn glamorous profession—*some* of the time. Yes, it all seems so irresistible when you see a model on television twirling around in some lavish outfit in front of a handsome cameraman she'll probably bed that night. *If only I had cheekbones and a clothing al-lowance,* you might think, *I could leave my husband and 2.5 children be-hind to pirouette around the windswept beaches of the Caribbean with*

Elle, Giselle, and all the other girls whose names end in a silent "e" and who claim to wear only mascara yet look fully made up at all times.

Working as a model, though, can be downright dangerous. There have been moments when I literally put my not-so-well-insured hide on the line to help a photographer get his shot—even when it could have been my *last* shot. If some photographer told me to roll around the ground and curl up with a man- (and woman-) eating tiger while looking at the beast with a lustful gaze, it never dawned on me that any normal person would have looked at the photo genius, pursed her very plump lips, and said, "What are you thinking? Are you out of your fucking *mind?*"

Now that I'm thinking again, the memories rush back in, and the modeling horror stories fill my head.

Swimming wit' da Fishes

Let's start back in the early 1970s. I remember working in Grenada on a proposed television series about models when the director told me, "Janice, you're going to get into a wetsuit and jump into the water for a brisk little swim." I grew up in Florida, so the swimming part wasn't a problem. The trouble was, I'd be swimming with a shark, one of the most dangerous creatures known to man.

Please! The only kind of sharks I knew drove BMWs in Hollywood; the only bites they left you with were emotional. On the other hand, a leopard shark's bite would have made for a pretty fine obit: "Janice Dickinson. Insane model. Stupid enough to get into that tank and swim with flesh-eating sharks. Her family and friends, who clearly think she was nuts, will miss her and her keen fashion sense."

When I heard that I might soon be joining the ocean's food chain, I was sent to wardrobe to find the perfect, sexy, hug-every-curve wetsuit. An hour later, I was covered in so much rubber I looked like a giant condom with a pair of 36C's sticking out the front. On my way over to the shark tanks, I had a strange feeling in the pit of my stomach—and it wasn't just my usual hunger pains.

"Janice, those sharks are virtually harmless," said the cameraman in charge of the shoot when he noticed the look of terror in my eyes. Of course, the only word I heard was *virtually*. But I just took a deep breath and hid my frightened feelings behind the black rubber mask I put on.

My part of the shoot required me to dive into the water with an oxygen tank on my back and then swim to the shark tank.

"Do you know how to dive?" the cameraman asked hopefully.

"Of course," I said, though in truth everything I knew about diving I learned from watching *Sea Hunt* as a kid. (No joke: every single day I came home from school to stare at handsome nature-man Lloyd Bridges, watching him save people from their own stupidity in the water. Where was Lloyd when I needed him today?)

After a dive that might have registered a 3.0 with the Olympic coaches, I paddled my way over to the shark tank, where a pair of steely eyes met my baby browns. We sized each other up, the way most models do at these shoots. Was he thinking, *I wonder if she got paid more than me?*

Nope. He was thinking, *Buffet!*

As Mr. Shark swam toward me, I pretended this was just another hotshot jerk trying to put the moves on me. Then I remembered: *I had my period.* Sharks. Blood. *Duh.* The voice of one of my elementary school nuns popped into my brain: "Sharks are prehistoric predators." That'll teach me to listen in school.

After waiting a few hundred hours, the underwater photographer finally swam over to take a few shots. Eventually, he gave me the thumbs-up sign and motioned for me to return to the surface. My finny new paramour tracked me a little bit on my way up. Men have never been able to leave me alone, no matter what their species.

At dinner the following night, my handsome businessman date leaned over and said to me, "Your job is so glamorous."

I just threw a bread roll at him—I wasn't planning on eating it anyway—and ordered the seafood combo.

Postscript: Years later, at a Beverly Hills party, I found myself in the company of Mr. Lloyd Bridges himself. I sashayed up to Mr. Sea Hunt, grabbed his hand, and said, "Lloyd, I just want to thank you for saving my life in Grenada." Lloyd glanced away at his wife, as if to say, "I've never been to Grenada, and I've never seen this woman in my life." Then I explained that I was a *Sea Hunt* fanatic.

"Did you go down?" Mr. Bridges asked. (For once, this was a question about *diving*.)

"Oh, I went down eighty-five feet," I replied, sipping my drink.

"Young lady, that's not very bright," he said.

"Because of you, Mr. B, I knew how to clear my mask and avoid getting eaten by a killer shark. I'll be grateful forever," I purred. I'm not sure, but I think Lloyd had a look of grandfatherly pride in his eyes. Years later, when I was on another shoot that required fins, I put them on with no glitches and whispered, "*Sea Hunt* rules!"

The Hard, Cold Truth

In the late 1980s, I was hired to strut my hot-mama stuff in a hot red bikini on the glossy pages of *Vogue*. My smile said, "Hey, baby, I'm revved up and ready to go." In the finished photos, steam seemed to be pouring from my every pore.

But here's the rub: that "summertime" shoot was shot on the coast of west Florida—in January. Magazines have to work about six months in advance to bring you that issue you have in your hot little hands.

Mike Reinhardt, the photographer for this bikini bonanza, chose Florida because he figured that Florida temperatures never dip below the seventies—even in the winter. I was thrilled to escape the deep freeze of New York, but my happiness was short-lived. When we arrived in Florida, a freak cold spell had settled in, with temperatures in the low thirties. Just flipping on the news was depressing. All you saw were farmers crying over their ruined orange crop.

Myself, I wasn't orange. Try green. Our shoot was on the beach, and with all that misty freezing water hitting my ninety-percent-naked bod, my skin was turning a morbid lime color that even the thickest makeup couldn't cover up. Between shots, I just huddled in nothing but a white terry cloth robe and va-va-voom string bikini, while my body was convulsing in epileptic shivers.

"Baby, I hate to do this, but drop the robe," Mike said after he set up for the first of many shots. Honestly, I think the goose bumps on my arms were bigger than my breasts.

"Think toasty! *Toasty!*" Mike said, smiling as he zipped his Columbia parka high around his neck and adjusted his cashmere scarf. As if somehow I could use my mental powers to melt the frostbite off my belly button. It was a nice plan, but useless. My teeth were chattering so hard I was sure I'd pop another cap.

"I'm so sssorrry," I tried to say through my blue, unusable lips.

Always the survivor, I came up with a plan to save the shoot. Racing inside our nearby hotel, I ran up to my room and put on my white Adidas.

Working for *Vogue*—those eight years were the pinnacle of my career.

Then I proceeded to run around the block . . . in the bikini. You can imagine the traffic I caused.

I ran like an Olympian, and eventually I became so hot and sweaty that I looked like I needed a cabana boy to fan me. Later that June, when the issue of the magazine came out, a friend of mine called. "My God! Janice, Florida looks so beautiful in the winter. I'm booking a vacation," she said.

"Bring a parka," I said.

Burning Babe

Of course, there's a flip side to every story—and this one takes place in New York's Central Park in June. One year, during an extraordinary heat wave, temps reached 105 in the shade; the air was so thick with humidity that I figured I might as well just let my hair frizz into a natural Afro. But that wasn't practical because Beverly Johnson, Patty Hansen, and I were working for a fur company, and I just couldn't allow myself to have a bad hair day. So the three of us gathered in the park, pulled on those hot

Yves St. Laurent #19. Don't leave home without it. Jerry Hall liked me then.

minks, and pretended we were so damn cold we needed thousands of dollars of fur to warm us up.

"Can you believe this, Janice?" Beverly groused when we arrived. "I won't even have to work out today—I sweated off three pounds just walking from the car to this clump of trees in the park!"

Meanwhile, I was taking the ice cubes out of my drink and rubbing them on my red face. It wasn't just the heat that was getting to me, but also my lifestyle at the time, which was a little too hot to handle. The night before the shoot I'd been up until three in the morning at Studio 54, and the combination of sleep deprivation and a minor hangover had me dragging.

"Are they insane? They want us to change outfits six times?" Patty griped, sweat dripping off her famous mug.

Meanwhile, I got out my own fishing-tackle-box-worth of makeup and went to work on the old kisser, which needed maximum help that day. What I could have used was a twenty-four-hour nap before being called to the set, but that wasn't going to happen.

After I put on a tight black number, the photographer's assistant walked over with what must have been about thirty dead foxes sewn together. It was the kind of coat that would allow anyone to survive winter in Alaska, in an igloo with no space heater and no cute Eskimo to keep things interesting.

"Does this come in a fur vest?" I joked. I knew the moment I put that full-length coat on I'd be doomed.

A few minutes later, I heard the words that filled me with dread: "Janice, we're ready for you," said the annoyingly pleasant assistant.

Bravely I slipped on the coat, as if I were the ultimate sinner taking her first few steps into the fiery pits of Hell. I remember staring at the photog, and gazing up at a big old elm tree. That's about all I recall.

The next thing I remember was a voice that seemed to be screaming at me from the back of my brain. "Janice! *Janice!* Are you alive?!" the photographer shrieked. When I opened my eyes, I found I had blades of grass stuck up my nose and dirt on my cheek. I'd passed out—over and out!

I never met a situation I didn't try to fix. So, as I struggled to my feet, I tried to suggest a setup change: "In this shot, my man has surprised me in Central Park with the most beautiful fur coat, and the thrill of it all makes me faint on the spot," I said hopefully.

"Someone get Beverly and clean Janice up," the photog instructed. "Give Beverly the fox coat. When Janice is ready, we'll put her in the fur-lined gloves."

"You know what goes well with fur gloves?" I suggested. "Me—naked."

Well, no one went for that one either, but at least I tried.

The Biggest Boobs of All

I went up for a Maidenform bra ad, and the audition was a bit over the top, even for me. In the privacy of a dressing room, the bra brass told me to try on a couple of strappy numbers. The next stop was a boardroom, where about twelve men sat around looking bored, which really amused me. A roomful of middle-aged men whose job was basically to stare at women's tits all day, suspended in their latest contraptions of torture. How many men would kill for this gig?

I think these assholes liked the power they had over the women who tramped through their Star Chamber, auditioning their boobs for glory. I wasn't about to give them the satisfaction of psyching me out. Nudist that I am, I stood there for five minutes in just a bra and skin-tight black pants while they discussed my rack like I wasn't even there.

"Don't you think she's a little small?" said one guy, five-foot-three with jowls down to his waist.

"I thought she had implants," said another moron in a ratty old leisure suit. Decades come and go, but I guess polyester is forever.

"Can we get someone younger?" another asked. I don't even think he was an executive with Maidenform; when I turned to eye him, he was putting out the second round of doughnuts.

Finally, I blew. Unhooking the bra, I placed my hands on both hips and tossed back my mane of dark hair. Eyeballs popping, the men were in various stages of heart failure when I whipped the bra across their carefully polished conference table.

"Take this bra and stick it up your asses!" I ranted. "You people have no idea of what's hot and what's not."

Harrumphing out of the room, I thought, *Don't these idiots know they can retouch my breasts in the actual ads? And how dare they talk about my body like I'm not even there? That's the same shit I got from . . . my father.* No woman should be subjected to that kind of treatment—certainly not as a defenseless girl, and absolutely not as a grown woman.

As an adult, though, I had one advantage: I could take my tits and hit the road. And that's just what I did.

Shitty Shutterbugs

It wasn't the camels that were snippy during a cigarette campaign I shot in the late 1970s for a very famous photographer who shall remain nameless. This guy was awfully grumpy and rude, and "his people," who'd been deputized by this asshole, all acted the same way. "You can boss the models around," he must have told them. "They're not here for a vacation."

What followed was the worst kind of verbal abuse. It certainly wasn't fun to be stuck in Morocco with a dictator whose only power was his lens. After four days of being told I was "stupid," "worthless," and "not fit for this ad," the photographer invited me out for dinner. Was he kidding?

I tried to decline—who needed more of this crap?—but he insisted. "You will have dinner with me, or you can get your ass back on the plane and go home."

Over the shrimp cocktails, he skipped the small talk and got right to the main course, which was to tell me everything that was wrong with my life. This was back in my drinking days, so two glasses of wine later, after I'd had enough of his tirades, I decided he deserved his just desserts.

"Look, I've worked with all the greats, and you are a *vile man!*" I said, standing up from the table like Joan Collins in *Dynasty.* "I don't take this kind of shit from anybody!" I screamed.

I wasn't just blowing smoke: when you pull a stunt like that, you've gotta mean it. I ditched the job and got on the next plane out of there. Sometimes the paycheck just isn't worth what you have to do to get it.

Photogs are a strange lot. I remember another Italian fashion shoot where the very famous European shutterbug (you know who you are) told me I should arrive at his studio at eight in the morning. I was there at eight on the dot, ready to shoot—but he was elsewhere, both mentally and physically.

I had to wait until well past six o'clock that evening for him to come down off his meth high. This guy practically held me, a Swedish and a French model, four assistants, two makeup artists, and a wardrobe woman hostage for an entire day, waiting for him to get his drug habit under control.

I could go on and on when it comes to photographers who should be shot by their models.

When I was very young, a photographer had me and six young girls do what would be the equivalent of a 10.0 Olympic backbend to prove that a certain brand of designer lingerie could be used for—what, yoga? I never understood it; all I knew was that my back was breaking, as he forced us to hold our backbends for longer than any human being should have to. I should have sent him the bill from my chiropractor.

Of course, the worst-case scenario is always the photographer who has some sort of porn fantasy of seducing his model. I can't tell you how many photographers tried to get me high on coke to get me "in the mood" for the shoot. Many girls are only too happy to comply in order to get the work, but I never jumped on the "will fuck for work" bandwagon.

Instead, I was one of the few who projected a definite "Don't fuck with me" vibe, and I meant it in every way possible. I certainly hope the mothers who are reading this book will think twice and insist on accompanying their young daughters to modeling auditions. I know that if my

Opposite: Iman Bowie backstage at a Calvin Klein show in Tokyo, Japan. She was into makeup way before anybody.

daughter, Savvy, ever wanted to try modeling, I'd be there if she were seventy-five and I was on life support. I'd follow her until I gasped my last breath because I know what happens at shoots gone shitty.

Ultimately, I believe I've got those bad shoots to thank for all those lines that cropped up on my face. Isn't it ironic to think I earned them in the modeling business? Luckily, now I can fix my face. If only I could Botox my memories.

Fortunately, a few of the horror stories actually ended with me smiling.

Men Will Be . . . Women?

One day, in the late 1980s, I was working the runway at a fabulous Terry Mugler fashion show. My (fellow) model for the day was a gorgeous model who also went by the name of Teri. She was tall, slinky, and gorgeous, with large breasts, stick-straight Cher-style blonde hair, and the flattest stomach I've ever seen. The only strange thing about Teri was that she refused to change in front of the other models. At first I figured she had issues from childhood. Maybe she was mortified by the locker room talk at her high school. Maybe she got her period in front of all the other girls, like in *Carrie.* Who knew? Whatever it was, Teri always grabbed her designer duds and hightailed it to the back rooms at shows to change in private.

I'd change in the middle of Park Avenue, but to each her own.

On the runway that day, I was up first, in a beautiful black wrap dress that hugged every curve. My new pal Teri was set to follow me in this sheer, raw silk, skintight pastel-rose evening dress—perfect for your average night out at the Academy Awards. Cameras blinded me as I walked the walk, and then I glanced at Teri, who sashayed behind me.

I'm not sure why, but my eyes just gravitated to her crotch and . . . well, there was an awful lot going on down there. It looked like she had a boner. My eyes widened as it dawned on me: Teri was a *he.*

I'd had no idea. Unfortunately for Teri, her dress was such a tight little fashion statement that underwear wasn't an option. And when one handsome male model caught Teri's beautiful eye, my poor friend got a little "can't help it" action suddenly stirring in his/her dress. Then the hunk waved hello to Teri—and *boooooiiiiiinnnnng*, Teri stood up at attention, for all the fashion world to see!

This was just way too much lust on parade for us all to handle—especially the poor designer, whose dress wasn't build to handle the male member in heat. I mean, there wasn't even room under there for a light breakfast, let alone the whole enchilada. But I couldn't blame poor Teri: to be honest, I wouldn't have minded a piece of that male model myself. *I wonder if I'll have to arm-wrestle Teri for our little stud after the show?* I wondered, smiling and posing.

But all's well that ends well: she/he eventually had a sex change, became a real girl, and married her boyfriend. Last time I checked they were living on a farm, with two adopted kids. I wonder if she still whips out that tight evening dress on cold winter nights.

5.

The Good Old Days
of Debauchery

I miss debauchery.

I was talking about this the other day with writer and director George Axelrod, the genius who gave us the classic film *The Secret Life of an American Wife*. Darling George was nursing a big tumbler of vodka while trying to sun himself to death at his ultrachic home in the Hollywood Hills.

"Don't you miss the old days, Jan?" he asked me, twirling his glass, mixing the booze around with his finger. I was nursing an Evian with a lime.

"Don't you miss debauchery?" he added, sitting up to slather himself with tanning oil. Even as I sat there under an umbrella, worrying about skin cancer, global warming, my children, my dogs, my bank account—everything under the sun—the answer was obvious.

"Oh God, George, I miss it," I replied, sighing loudly. "I should have been born in the Roaring Twenties. I would have made some gangster a very well-dressed moll."

I was born a few years later, which meant that I lived out my own form of debauchery with all the perks of the 1970s. I practically lived at Studio 54, a place where drug-addled girls bent over the bar snorting party favors as some sleazoid took them from behind. We chased down the sex, drugs, and drinking with drinking, drugs, and sex. And I don't remember anyone having a problem with the menu.

Our party-hearty MO carried over to the fashion industry, where all of the above was encouraged. There were times when it was considered appropriate to come to a shoot high, or get high while you were there. In the disco era, you could either live in the fast lane or sit it out on the sidelines and wish you were there. I preferred to keep things revved up.

What a difference a few decades make. Now, instead of hanging at Studio 54, there are fifty-four whining kids in my daughter's sixth-grade class who need me to bake 'em some cupcakes for the PTA. (Me—bake? Who would have thought?!)

Now, instead of partying like a demon, I work like a demon on everything—my children, my dogs, my house, my career, and of course, myself. The madness continues, but it's just not as much fun as it used to be. Now it's all about this nonstop drive to maintain what I have. Where's the fun in that?

What happened to those days when it was all about highs and lows, drugs and parties, and those three little words—*sex, sex, sex?*

The sad truth is, I was the girl who went out dancing every single night, but stayed at the party just a little too long. I thought I needed all that craziness to keep going, but I was just trying to fill a void. I didn't know where I was going, but I couldn't stop. Now, with the help of my family, my friends, my therapist, and my friends at AA, I know something that's life-changing: *I'm enough.*

But it wasn't always that way.

Opposite: The gang in Aspen, getting ready for a perfect snowball fight!

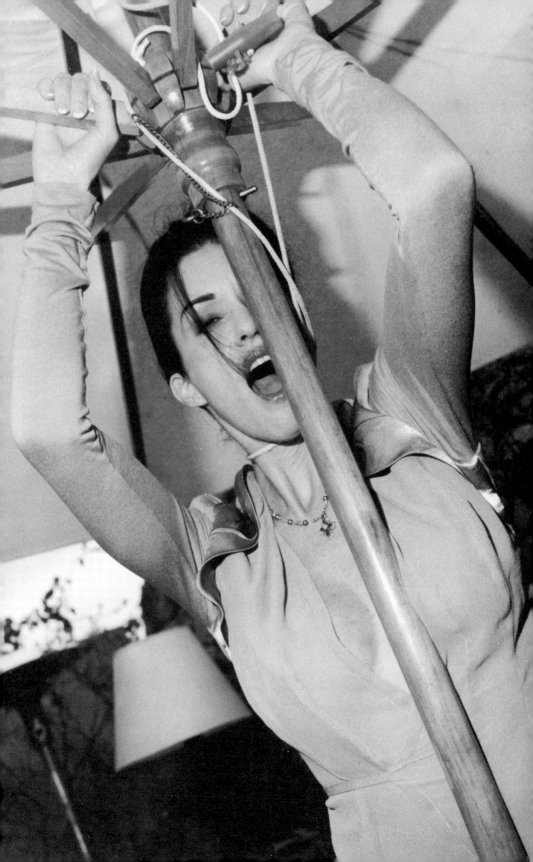

Once upon a time, my life was far more opulent. I had a starring role in my own version of *Lifestyles of the Rich and Famous*. I jetted off to the far reaches of the earth for events so spectacular they belonged in a Jackie Collins novel.

In the rock-'em-sock-'em 1980s, for example, I once attended a wedding in Jakarta. The attendees? A small crowd of the couple's closest friends—all 4,000 of them.

Oh, you want specifics? The son of the minister of defense was marrying my friend Djody's daughter. You want to talk about glamour? I saw more jewels at this wedding than Harry Winston hauls out of the vault at Oscar time. These women looked like human chandeliers.

Twinkling away on the star-studded guest list was Julia Roberts, who I ran into on the bathroom line. The poor girl looked a little tired; she'd just gotten back from the jungles of Bali, where she was filming some gorilla special for PBS. (God, hadn't she been pawed enough in the movies?) Maybe rolling around with the monkeys was good for her because Julia was sweet to everyone. She makes twenty mil a movie, lets monkeys spit in her hair, and she's nice to models! Can I adopt this girl?!

Jules and I partied down with the 4,000 other revelers that night. We danced, drank, got ogled by international billionaires, and more than once mentioned that our lives were a bit too much—even for us. "I'm from Georgia," she said. "What am I supposed to make of all this?"

"I've never seen this kind of spread in my entire life," I said. I didn't even mention that I was some punky kid who spent her summers working in a sweltering pizza parlor in the middle of Bumfuck, Florida.

That was only one of many times, though, when the madness was all around me. During my supermodel days, even a simple act like shopping took on a certain wicked twist.

Back in the day, the nicest designers would allow the models to keep one or two of their favorite items after a show. It was one of the best perks

Opposite: Pole dancing!

of the job because these pieces were one-of-a-kind creations. Certain girls accepted these gifts gracefully; others, like Jerry Hall, would brag endlessly about how they got a great pair of boots or a $1,000 pair of heels for free.

At the height of my own debauchery, though, Janice Dickinson took it a step too far—and once walked out of a Chanel show with *an entire rack* of clothes. Thank God those racks were on wheels. The backstage workers must have thought I was just being helpful, wheeling the rack out of the dressing room—and down the ramp and across the street, where I slipped my hotel doorman a healthy tip to bring it to my room. Later, I paid the maid another handsome tip to pack up "my new clothes" and ship them to my home.

At one Hermès show, I wheeled another rack of *haute couture* down the hallway and into the elevator when no one was looking. This time it was a little trickier because my hotel wasn't across the street—it was clear across town. Sure, it was pretty uncomfortable pushing that rack through the cobblestone streets of Paris, but I considered it a new form of cardio. (It was certainly much more interesting than the Stairmaster.) What's funny is, the few times I pulled off these heists, no one said a word. I'm not sure if they admired my bravado, or just enjoyed the fact that someone who really loved the clothes would be wearing them.

In my own defense, I was a very complimentary thief. When a crowd of reporters asked me about my Giorgio Armani dress, I said, "There is a certain *free*dom in wearing Gucci."

"How much does that leopard jacket cost?" a fashion scribe once asked.

"I truly can't put a price tag on it," I smiled.

Eat your heart out, Winona!

Nowadays, all that delicious, reckless self-indulgence has been replaced by the glaze of normal life. Am I happier now? Maybe, maybe not. Today, I gasp at how models traffic in the mundane. We risk breaking our very expensive acrylic nails just to pump our own gas—which reminds me of a little tale that proves my point.

The story begins on a hot day in Southern California. Let me tell you, the hottest visual I've seen recently is Miss Amber Valetta pumping gas at the Union 76 in Brentwood, sporting her trademark ice-blue Juicy track-suit and a big smile.

Is Amber living a life of debauchery? Well, I peeked in the backseat of her car, and it was full of evidence to the contrary—including a soccer ball and a darling black Marc Jacobs bag. To me, Amber is the reigning queen of supermodels these days—and there she was, living the suburban life just like the rest of us. What's next? Iman hawking cookies at a bake sale? Claudia shopping at Target?

Of course, there might be just a little debauchery left in Amber; apparently she isn't quite perfect, either. As I walked by the front end of her new Mercedes, I spotted a little dent. "As you know, Amber, supermodels can't drive," I told her. She just smiled that million-dollar grin. Afraid I might have offended her, I added, "I'm just kidding."

"No, Janice, you were right the first time," she said. "I was coming home from this wild . . ." I won't tell her story; it belongs to Amber. It might not qualify as debauchery, exactly, but Amber convinced me that there's still a little naughty fun left out there—which is perfectly good news, if you ask me.

6.

Dealing with Backbiting Bitches (Even the Ones in Your Own Mind)

I love my fellow models. Take Christie Brinkley. I used to marvel at how beautiful she was back in the day, that Christie.

Are we models really that competitive? Well, it's like asking if world leaders really get along, or if Martha Stewart is a nice gal. Come on! It doesn't matter whether I've ever met some particular model—if I start getting the idea that she's prettier, sexier, smarter than I am, I'm going to hate her. (Okay, maybe not smarter . . .) I bet most girls who spend time paging through the photos in the fashion mags do the same thing.

The other day, like any red-blooded American woman, I looked in the mirror and for a moment I didn't like what I saw. My first thought? *Maybe I need to look more like Amber, or Heidi, or Gisele.* Then I stopped myself in my tracks. "What are you thinking? You're forty-seven years old! What do you *want* from yourself?"

The answer is simple: Even at my age, when I look in the mirror, sometimes I think, "I'm just an alien from another planet. End of story." It takes me a minute to remind myself that it's not all falling apart. *Oh, right,* I think—*who the hell am I fooling?!*

Well, we tell ourselves we're trying to fool men, of course. But I don't blame the men. There's an even greater force out there that makes us want to strive to be better than the best. Of course, I'm talking about other women. How much do we really want to knock the socks off the other chicks? On a scale of one to ten, I'd give it about a twelve. In our quest for perfection, women can be our best friends, or our worst nightmare. When we're not trying to beat other women in some existential beauty race, we're trying to endear ourselves to them, by any means necessary. And that isn't easy for one simple reason: women can be such bitches to each other.

The other morning, for instance, I was taking Savvy to school when one of the other mothers approached me. "So, Janet," she said, "I see you're doing *More* magazine now—*for older women.*"

I already knew that this woman didn't like me because I don't fit into her cookie-cutter vision of a Stepford suburban soccer mom. "Excuse me," I said. "My name is *Janice,* and I'm a supermodel. And, yes, I happen to have a two-page layout in *More,* which makes me very proud." Then I shot her a lingering glance, as if to say, "Maybe you could get an audition, too. Where? How about Dairy Queen's annual report?"

Even your best female friends can be a challenge if you're feeling hormonal—which for me is about twenty-eight days of the month. About ten years ago, I was walking down 59th Street in New York when Christie, old flat-butt herself (honey, it's a *joke!*), and one of her husbands—I'm pretty sure it was the French one—were standing there looking in the window of some chic little store. Her baby blues locked with my baby browns, and I waved as I ducked into the *très* expensive Plaza Hotel as if I were staying there.

A minute later I popped back out—and they were still there. *Curses! Foiled again.* But I just sucked it up, walked up to Christie and French

Boy, and we all air-kissed. Couldn't they have walked faster so we could have avoided each other?

"Oh, I just had to give one of my packages to Roberto at the desk," I said. "I'm staying there for a month, and they're being *so* attentive." Christie's mouth dropped a bit as I droned on about my suite, my jobs, and my burning desire to hit the Chanel store on Fifth Avenue, where my stylist was holding a few outfits for my approval.

Lies, lies, lies. (I was going to Hell anyway.)

The point is, that little green jealous whore-mone that lives within all us women wants nothing more than to drive all other members of our gender nuts.

There are times when having other women "mess around in our business" seems as revolting as dating a guy with private parts the size of my little finger. Like the time my sister Alexis came out and asked me point-blank if I had fake tits.

"Janice, those can't be real," Alexis gasped, ogling me in the Bloomingdales dressing room as we tried on Saturday-night party clothes. When I saw her look of disapproval, I just rolled my eyes. "Please! I just dropped a kid, remember? You gain weight when you're pregnant, right? Now would you please go out and get me this dress in a fucking size six?" When she was gone, I checked my fake tits in the mirror and fell in love with them all over again.

When I find myself getting a bit too snippy with other chicks, I try to stop and focus on something else: washing my car, cleaning my pet, grooming myself, exercising, doing a little skin care, hair care, pussy care—anything to call a cease-fire in that lifelong battle between women to one-up each other. Sometimes I have to do all of the above just to get through the morning without a skirmish.

Models have one age-old way to show each other up, which leads me to the number-one question people always ask me: do models have sex with powerful men to get a leg up on their model competitors?

Is the sky blue? Does Manolo Blahnik have a sale only once a year?

People always ask me if models have to sleep their way to the top. The truth of the matter is, some girls blow it—to avoid blowing what they think may be their only opportunity for work.

Sometimes the sex can take a strange twist—even for this twisted industry. I'm reminded of the time a Brazilian model showed up a few minutes early for an interview to represent a major clothing line. It was up to a certain very famous photographer to put in "a good word" for the woman he thought would be the best face for the job.

Meanwhile, Miss Brazil had spent the entire morning in one of New York's priciest salons making sure she looked perfect. This wasn't enough, so she blew a wad of dough on the sexiest La Perla bustier, and vintage jeans that fit her like they were sewn on by a surgeon. She was feeling confident when she arrived at the photographer's studio, and didn't even think it strange that there was no one there to greet her. Making her way through the cavernous space, she sashayed toward the faint sound of voices in the office. As she approached the frosted glass, she didn't need to walk that close to witness a scene that is repeated in countless studios across the world.

What Brazil didn't expect was that a very famous model was there pleading her own case for this photographer—who, besides being a genius at his profession, was also one of the biggest hound dogs in the business. In fact, his favorite pose for auditioning models was on their knees. This particular model was known for her willingness to do "anything and everything," and this day was no exception. In other words, it wasn't going to be about the jobs she'd done in the past. It would be about the "jobs" she could perform on a one-on-one, here-and-now basis.

"Baby, keep going," the photographer moaned as Miss Brazil lingered outside the door, trying to resist the temptation to burst through the doors and ruin the moment.

But her self-control didn't last long. What happened next was like the Bermuda Triangle of auditions: the horny, the hungry, and the hissy fit. Seems our little friend from Brazil had a bit of an anger-management problem. To the other model's great misfortune, when our horny photographer had invited her into his private office, she'd left her portfolio, coat, purse, and everything else in the waiting room. Fortunately, his secretary was out for lunch when Brazil arrived.

After she realized what was going on behind closed doors, Brazil wasn't about to leave; hell, she'd come this far, and besides, that outfit cost a mint. What to do? As soon as she noticed the other model's portfolio on the table near the exit, revenge took hold. She took a tube of Crazy Glue out of her nail kit, tucked neatly in her Yves Saint Laurent summer tote. With the swiftness of an artist, she placed one little swish of glue on

Looking way too tough!

every single page—ruining thousands of dollars of priceless, irreplaceable work that the other model would need if she ever expected to get another job that wasn't a blow job.

Brazil sighed and left, satisfied in the knowledge that one little tube of glue had turned into an investment in her future.

Man-Stealers

When it comes to being mean, models don't just fight over jobs—sometimes they go woman-to-woman in death duels. Take Christie, who seems to be all over this chapter. (Of course, I only tell these stories with love.) But those of you who've been paying attention throughout my career might recall that Christie took off with my then-boyfriend, photographer Mike Reinhardt. The very day after I dumped Mike, she moved in with him. The man didn't even spend twenty-four hours without a supermodel in his bed, which might just be a world record. As for Christie and me? Well, the episode didn't exactly cement our friendship.

The sad thing is, we'd genuinely *been* friends before all that went down. I even had to ask myself, *What is she thinking? Is she trying to emulate my feelings for this man? Is she trying to be me?*

It occurred to me that some so-called girlfriends could be so self-seeking that they wouldn't consider the feelings of the woman standing there in the stilettos next to her before acting. It's not a perfect world— please, I know that much—but shouldn't there be certain unspoken rules and boundaries among girlfriends of all ages, professions, and creeds?

For instance, let's say I have designs on a film director whose last movie made $125 million at the box office and who was just signed to a three-picture deal at Paramount. Of course, I'll talk about him with my girlfriend, giving her a daily briefing on the latest events (e-mails, phone calls, "accidental" meetings at restaurants). But I'm doing that under one basic, understood guideline: *Hey, girl, I'm only letting you in on this because I know you're not going to cross the boundaries of female loyalty by trying to sink your talons into my man, right?*

That's the law of the jungle—in a perfect world.

Women who violate this law aren't friends. They're bitches to beware of in the future. Erase them from your speed-dial and spread the word: they're not to be trusted.

Of course, some scenarioes aren't exactly cut and dried. Let's say you're at a club and both you and your girlfriend notice the same stud at the exact same moment. You both think he's hot; you'd both like to wake up the next morning and find him under your Calvin Klein comforter. What do we do? After all, we're not men, we can't punch each other out for the prize, or flip a coin, or arm-wrestle.

Hello? Janice Knows All. The only honest thing to do in this situation is to get out a tube of Chanel mascara and spin it on top of the bar. I've actually done this with other models at various hot Los Angeles clubs, and it works like a charm. If it points to you, you get to approach the guy. In a pinch, you can accomplish the same result by flipping a Chanel compact. Think of it as the upscale version of a coin toss: if the two C's land faceup, I'm the one who approaches Mr. Studliness.

Men often complicate this sort of international dating democracy. They can also ruin potential friendships between models and civilians alike. After Sly Stallone did his bam-slam-ham action with me and then gave me "das boot," he hooked up with the first girl he could find: thirteen hours later he was engaged to redheaded model Angie Everhart. I truly believe Sly did this mostly to hurt my feelings—although, for the record, I didn't really give a rat's ass. Back then, he behaved as if he had a retractable deal with a diamond dealer, where he could hang onto a nice engagement ring long enough to see if it stuck, and then snatch it back and return it if things went south. I'm surprised he doesn't give them out attached to a Slinky.

Club Sluts

There's a particular breed of big-city model who've managed to convince themselves they're living the perfect life—largely because they only come out in the dark. Recently, purely for research purposes, I decided to investigate their kind and see if they really have a line on the best of all possible lives.

Allow me to introduce you to the girls I call the Club Sluts.

Ladies, you know who you are. These club sluts are the female, new-millennium version of John Travolta in the vintage film *Saturday Night Fever*. These chicks work all day (most only claim to be models), but the one thing that's really important to them is that when the sun goes down and the lights go up, they're out there shaking their booties all over town.

Not long ago, I worked with one of them on a modeling shoot. It was a lingerie shoot, but it seemed more like the opening of some lesbian porn film. Picture this: her hands wrapped around my waist, settled a few inches under my tits. I'm not exactly sure what we were selling, but whatever it was, I knew men would be lining up around the block to buy it. *(Pantyhose? Great! Send a crate! Midol? Bring it on!)*

It was a long, long day, though—because this bitch kept grabbing me in all my ticklish zones. Even worse, I had to listen to her fucking drone on and on about how she not only lived in the clubs at night, but was also a hand model by day, so she had to protect herself at all times with gloves. She even drank at night with gloves on.

"Oh, you're so fab," I lied. Hoping to cut the conversation short, I added, "I always slather up my feet and hands to keep them soft, so I could give you a few tips." Undeterred, she went on to tell me her entire life story, including how working as a hand model was the only way to pay for her clubbing at night, which was her *real* life. *Now* I was interested. Clearly this was a new social phenomenon.

Since she was only a hand model, I thought it strange that she didn't eat anything for eight hours, and kept popping diuretics like candy. "You need a completely flat stomach for the clubs," she told me. What kind of social life was this? It was more like her job.

A few weeks later, I decided to join some New York club sluts for a few nights of clubbing like mad, and kept a mental diary of their most perfect clubbing tips.

"Janice, the only thing you ought to drink is Red Bull. It'll help you lose weight at the club. It's better than the gym. With all that dancing, you'll walk out two pounds lighter," one clubbie insisted.

My God! I thought. *Why doesn't someone write a book about this new weight-loss plan?* Just shimmying around in those heels was enough to rev up my metabolism and tone my calves at the same time. For a moment I did curse the fact that I ever quit smoking; all these other girls used cigs as a way to curb their appetites.

"You don't smoke?" one cried. I hated to tell her, but the smell was making me want to puke.

There are times when you just have to haul your now-smarter ass home, get away from the other bitches, and consider yourself lucky to have survived it all. As far as I'm concerned, those club sluts don't have to worry about another girl trying to squeeze into the pack. This lone wolf prefers to step out when the sun is shining.

Male Models Mania

I'd like to interrupt this chapter and switch genders for a moment. As if the girls aren't bad enough, there's a new breed out there called "the male model." Once upon a time, they used to be known as just "good-looking guys." Now they have contracts and cosmetic deals.

I've dated a few of these men, and the good news is that they stare at themselves in the mirror less than Warren Beatty. But it's strange to go out with a man who draws more stares than you do when you enter a room—I'm talking lustful gazes from both women and men.

At one point, I was dating hot-hottie-hot male model Bob Menna, who had jet-black hair, thick eyebrows, and a chiseled bod that would put Superman's to shame. Bob was sweet, but going out with him was a pain in the ass. At restaurants, the waitresses could hardly write or speak, they were so busy drooling over Bob. They'd stand there stammering, stuttering, practically falling to their knees. "Honey, *hello!*" I'd wave. "Over here? *I'll have the salad?*" After a while they'd have to call in the paramedics to revive the poor girl. Such was the power of Bob.

My friend Charlie Haugh, another male model, looked like a young Marlon Brando, but that was only part of his charm. Charlie had this way of greeting you that announced from the get-go he was a physical guy. I mean, what else can you make of a Greek statue of a man who meets you and two seconds later throws you up in the air, where you flip gracefully before landing in his huge, muscular, tanned arms? Charlie was like an amusement park ride with a penis: ride at your own risk, and enjoy at all costs.

These days, male supermodels like Marcus Shakenbacon (my pet name for Marcus Schenkenberg) get paid a king's ransom for each shoot. But you can't begrudge them the cash. They seem to have an even shorter shelf life than most female models. Honestly, I think we girls get bored too easily with them: we start craving our new hunk as soon as we're used to the old one.

I have noticed that male models aren't as bitchy as the females when it comes to their own gender. You don't often find them trying to one-up the other guys. Usually they're trying to one-up the girls, but in a playful way.

I admit, it's a little strange to sip designer water with the current It Man who is just as interested as you are in the latest face cream or the hottest hair product. Of course, a lot of male models also like to talk about their rod oil—enough said. I guess there are times when it's good to be a woman. (One less product to buy!) I've had many discussions with male models about hair removal, and believe me, that's a sensitive topic for them, too. Given that men are bigger babies about what's going on down there, I've suggested therapy, and my own personal waxer, to a few of my favorite male models. If you care, you share.

If only women could adopt that motto.

7.

The Perfect
Career Comeback

It all began when Tyra Banks, bombshell extraordinaire, got her well-manicured hands on my first book. And I didn't need to ask her for a mini-review: there she was on the other end of my cell phone, cooing, "Janice, I need you!"

(For purposes of historical accuracy: Not *that* way. Get your mind out of the gutter—or turn around and get back to the "Are All Models Lesbians?" chapter.)

This was strictly business—but a major career turn for me. Turns out, Tyra was producing, starring in, and casting *America's Next Top Model*, her own reality show about the making of a new supermodel. She was looking for judges. And she was looking for *me*.

"Can you come to my office to discuss?" Tyra asked. Then she mentioned that I could be to her model search what Simon Cowell was to *American Idol*. I jumped in my car and got on the road. Yes, Trya needed someone who was rough, tough, and had seen enough to tell it straight. I was absolutely head over heels about the prospect of working with

Ms. Extraordinaire, where I would be judging these young model-wannabes. Or, as Tyra said, "Be your usual opinionated self, honey!"

My meeting with Tyra for this gig lasted about twelve seconds—the swat of a fake eyelash. I was in awe of Ms. Banks; she dug me, too; and I got the job on the spot.

First, I had to return to prep for my big TV comeback. After scheduling a manicure and a wax, I found myself on Doheny Drive in Beverly Hills with one of Tyra's stylists buying a new Jackie O dress and some fabulous Christian Louboutin wraparounds for the first night of filming. Next, I stopped by my friend Nick Chavez's salon and began throwing his products into my large shopping bag. Nick was amused when it was clear I wasn't going to pay for any of it. Then I went home and packed so many clothes it looked like I was moving to New York forever—which is about how long the eight weeks on location felt.

In the limo to LAX, I was still wondering, *Do I have enough shoes?* The poor porter carrying my luggage out of the car had to take small breaks so he wouldn't collapse at the curb. I gave him an extra twenty dollars to clean the sweat off his brow.

The particulars included me moving into a New York hotel for eight weeks, leaving my kids behind in L.A. (it really broke my heart—I called them ten times a day), so I could judge ten young girls who would have given their (mostly) fake boobs to be proclaimed the next big model-perfect thing. These little babes were put in a hotel penthouse suite, under the cameras twenty-four-seven. Our job as judges was to evaluate the test shoots Tyra staged, to test their beauty, style, and strength of spirit.

From the start, it was like entering a time warp for me. The only thing I could see on these nymphs was the hunger in their eyes. I reeked of that same hunger when I first started out; I *remembered* that feeling of wanting to make it so badly it hurt. It wasn't just about the money, but the validation. I wanted to know I was worth it.

God—it never changes, I thought.

But it wasn't my job to provide social commentary. I was there to say things like, "Simplify your look," or "That dress makes you look like you just got run over by a Mack truck," or "When I think of roots, I want to re-member the TV miniseries, not the ugly crap growing out of your head." Tyra would eyeball me when I'd get real with the girls, but she knew it was all true, true, true. We only had eight weeks to send someone skyrocketing from obscurity to fame in our own version of model boot camp.

Fasten your bra straps—it was going to be a bumpy ride.

I love it that there was so much controversy over the first episode of the show, where the girls got their snatches waxed. For those who didn't tune in, a waxer was sent to the model-wannabes' hotel suite, then informed them all that they had a few minutes to drop their drawers and spread 'em, in preparation for the ultimate Brazilian bikini wax.

It was hilarious: all ten girls poking their legs up in the air nervously as if they were at the gynecologist's office. You could see the looks of fear in their eyes as the woman zeroed in on their parts with a bowl of hot, bubbling wax and the world's largest Popsicle stick. I heard one girl actu-ally screaming for her mother—and another who seemed to like it and wanted another go.

Does this support what I've been saying all along in this book or what? Beauty is pain. Those girls were lucky to experience their agony at the hands of the fabulous J Sisters of New York. Yes, you must agonize for your beauty; pouring hot wax on your snatch is just part of the price you pay to be a new-millennium woman.

The simple fact is, *everyone* must de-hair these days. Men need to get rid of that ugly, disgusting back hair; women must get rid of anything that resembles a Chia Pet growing on their bodies. Any hair that's not on the head is not to be tolerated. I can't help thinking of Madonna during her Danceteria days: before the Material Girl got it together and started re-moving the hair from her pits, she had the most vicious odor coming from I don't even want to know where. Believe me, it was no holiday dancing next to Madonna way back then.

And it was no holiday for the girls on *America's Next Top Model*, either. From photo shoots to media training, the girls had to undergo a series of tests to see if they had "It." Once a week they all were evaluated and one was eliminated. It paid to stick around because the ultimate prize was a modeling contract with Revlon, a contract with Wilhelmina, and a *Marie Claire* spread. Priceless spoils.

Our first test found the girls on the roof of a New York high-rise, where they would model bathing suits in eight-degrees-below-zero weather. After the episode aired, I was asked, "Janice, didn't you feel bad for the girl with zero percent body fat? She was shaking so violently, I thought she was having a seizure." Uh-uh, girls: only the strong survive. Believe me, I've worked on plenty of frigid rooftops wearing nothing but a thong. Hell, I've rolled in the snow wearing a string bikini. You've got to risk being a little cold if you want to be hot.

As for the behavior of the models, I was appalled that several girls couldn't get their asses out of bed and make it to their first photo shoot on time. Tyra, always on the ball, scolded them. The Big Dog (moi) would have gone ballistic and made them go a week without a manicure or pedicure. Seriously, I was disgusted. At photo shoots like this one—which was for J. Lo's new swim line—tens of thousands of dollars are riding on each minute. If you're late, you're dead. In the real modeling world, these tardy airheads would have been sent home with a black mark against their names. Sleep in, and you're out.

Am I being harsh? Honey, this is what I do!

Not long after that, I found myself sitting in a makeup chair with a bunch of other industry types, including Marcus "the Hottie" Schenkenberg. No matter what Marky Mark might like to think about dropping trou for Calvin Klein, Marcus was the first male supermodel; hell, he was the bomb. Now here I was sitting next to him, with his six-pack abs and his tight little buns.

Opposite: Here I'm thinking that I have no idea what expression to make. Every model goes through this.

"So yummy," I whispered to one of the other models. "There are times when I have to remind myself, *You have a boyfriend. Yes, you do . . . You should call him . . . Don't get in trouble, Janice.*" Was it my fault that I couldn't find my cell phone?

But things got decidedly not-so-yummy during one episode of the show, when I ran into one of the women in this business who clearly hates my guts. There I was, face to face again with Eileen Ford, the owner and founder of the famed Ford Modeling Agency.

When I was starting out, I would have held the loose skin on her face while they lifted it if she'd only given me just a glance. (Poor Eileen looks like her face has been lifted so many times she has begun to resemble the Joker after a hard night of partying around Gotham.) It's pretty safe to say she isn't my biggest fan, either. It's all on the record: I stormed out of her agency in the 1970s, refusing to sign with her—which in the long run cost her serious dough. No wonder Eileen has "a problem" with *moi.* Even before the show started, she was already spewing nasty comments about me behind my back. Unfortunately, I overheard her talking about me during one particular shoot—and somehow, as nasty as she was, it was nice to know that after all these years Eileen still had a real hard-on for the world's first supermodel.

"I heard *she's* in the building," I heard her whisper to a snippy-looking bottle blonde. "And I want to say that Janice Dickinson is a liar." The blonde, some TV exec, looked only too happy to insert herself in the middle of a good old-fashioned verbal catfight.

I should have slapped that weathered bitch. But I held back.

Instead of having some sort of confrontation, though, I went about my *America's Next Top Model* business. Then, after we wrapped for the day, I walked several miles home just to let off some steam. Sure, it was great to be back in the limelight, but it was also a slap in the face. Apparently the old days of industry backbiting were still alive and well.

Back on the set, finding the new face of beauty proved to be tougher than it looked.

First of all, I'm old-school; I've had chronic punctuality disease since *way* back in the day. So I was Ja-not-so-nice when one of the other judges, Mrs. Kimora Lee Simmons (the face of Chanel and owner of the Baby Phat clothing line), made the rest of us judges wait around on the set forever for her to pull up in her brand-new Bentley and grace us with her presence.

Kimora, who says she was a model for Karl Lagerfeld, waltzed onto our soundstage in midtown Manhattan wearing approximately one million dollars on each finger. The girl had more bling bling than any one girl ought to be allowed to carry, all thanks to her husband, Def Jam honcho Russell Simmons. On that first day, Kimora and I sized each other up like two wolves in heat. For a moment I thought she liked me—when she saw me noticing her jewelry. But I didn't want to talk about her loot; I've always thought it's in poor taste to go on and on about your newly acquired possessions. (Can you say *nouveau riche*? Can you say *pain in the ass?*)

"And then Russell bought me this ten-carat diamond, bling-bling-bling," Kimora gushed, blinding me with the shiny boulder. It was all I could do to bite my tongue and not rock the boat. Still, I didn't hold back all the way.

"Yeah, that's a nice ring," I said with a sigh. "You must have fun spending your husband's cash. Now, get your ass in the makeup room. We've been waiting for about two days."

Meanwhile, Tyra had put together an amazingly diverse group (sort of) when it came to the contestants whose very lives were on the line here. My mouth was also on the line, in ways I never expected.

"Do we have enough Oriental girls, Tyra?" I asked, sweetly.

"*Asians*, Janice," a producer corrected me with a frown. While waiting for Kimora (what else was new?), I pointed out that I knew the 'hood better than anyone. "I was practically born black," I reminded them all.

"*African-American*, Janice," the producer corrected me.

"God, excuse *me*," I said. "I've never been down with political correctness, and this is no time to start."

Walking around those land mines, I sat in the judges' pit as we waited to meet the remaining girls. I thought it was interesting that Tyra added a plus-size model who kept surviving each week's cut. Perhaps that's truly because the shape of America is changing, but the show wasn't called *America's Next Plus-Size Supermodel.* So I don't necessarily think I was being mean when I told our plump princess to pass on the mashed potatoes and fried chicken at the Sunday picnics.

I'm sorry if that sounds brutal, but I'm just being honest—the same way I was on the show. Since then I've received e-mails asking, "Janice, how could you have been so mean to some of those girls—especially the larger-sized girl?" Sure, I was opinionated on the show, but that's why I was hired. As for the plus-size girl, she *was* a beautiful woman—but if she wants to work as a model, she's going to have to learn to keep her appetite in check. I'm not the one who made up these rules, but I had to live with them just like everybody else.

I did her a favor; what I said was *nothing* compared to what she would hear at modeling agencies. When you're a model, your job is to work really hard on yourself, and this girl needed a little bit more devotion to that aspect of the job. Believe me, I felt her pain. Don't you think there are still days when I'd like to devour a five-course meal, too? Of course, I loved how others busted me for saying kind things about the extremely thin girl with the pixie haircut. "Ooooh, she's too tiny," the other models whispered. "She looks like a boy." Excuse me? I was 119 pounds in my prime; this girl weighs 114. All those bitches whining about her weight were just jealous. The girl was a born waif, and like it or not, that look sells. It certainly didn't hurt Kate Moss, who's so thin she could fall through the slats of a bench.

There were times on the show when I had to be equally honest with the other girls when it came to their bodies. "Your face is good—but size eleven feet? Bad!" I told one of the women, who looked like she had scuba fins permanently attached to her ankles. To another thin girl, I suggested, "You gotta work on those thighs. It's not all about your gorgeous face. It's about the booty, too."

"You've chosen the wrong profession," I informed one girl, who glared back through ten inches of gloppy mascara. I think they had to steam her eyes open in the morning.

The network suits were loving it. They even called a big meeting to tell me they wanted me to be an even bigger ballbuster to the girls. Naturally, I wouldn't be told what to do. "I'll say exactly what I want," I replied evenly. "I won't hurt anyone just for the sake of ratings. I won't bend and salivate, either, like Lorenzo Lamas on *Are You Hot?*" I spent one episode telling the girls to "remain true to yourself, even if you get booted from this show." I got a dirty look from my fellow judges when I told the hopefuls: "Our opinions mean nothing if you believe in yourself. Fight to get where you want. Take no prisoners!"

I did exactly that when the show moved to Paris for a few days. Deciding to ignore my detractors, I had a blast hosting a huge dinner party for my old model friends. I wore the most beautiful YSL short black dress, and we had a lovely meal before rocking the night away at three French discos. I had no idea I was still so famous. When a horde of people started dancing around me at the last club—there must have been close to a hundred, all eyes focused on me—I asked one of them what the hell was going on.

"We're Janice groupies," one gorgeous *garçon* confided. It was quite heavenly.

I flashed back to one night back in the 1970s when I could have used a few groupies. In search of a little gender-bending fun, I went to a French disco dressed entirely like a boy, in a black suit, with my hair slicked back and a pencil-thin mustache glued onto my upper lip.

At around 3:00 A.M.—after dancing the night away with beautiful members of both sexes—I went outside and got in a cab. The obviously gay driver drove a block, then caught a glimpse of pretty-boy me in the rearview mirror and said the words that Janice *usually* loves to hear: "*Voulez-vous couchez avec moi?*"

"*Non,*" I said. And when I did, he whipped around with rage and punched me in the face.

"But I'm a *girl!*" I cried. Before I knew it, though, he'd pulled over and kicked me out of the cab. Sitting on a bench near the Louvre, with a trickle of blood running down my fake mustache, I realized that maybe guys didn't have it so perfect, either.

Luckily, no blood was shed during our Paris shoot for *America's Next Top Model.* I was having a grand time being back in the sway.

Back in New York, the real nastiness (and hilarity) actually happened among the judges. During one episode, I looked at Kimora's hideously long nails and said, "Wow—obviously *you* don't type." She was dumbfounded. I took a more direct approach: "Hey, Miss Thing, trim those hooker nails. Mine are fake, but at least they're good fakes." By the next episode, Kimora's were clipped down to the quick.

During one of the shoots, I put my still-fabulous gams up on the judge's table in my trademark sexy pose. "Your age spots are showing," snipped Kimora.

Ah—Miss Thing wanted to take *me* on? Was she going to be sorry . . .

"Kimmy, I love your hair weave. But did you intend for it to look like the cheap fake fur they sell at Wal-Mart? Can't you pawn one of those rings and go to a real salon?"

She just gasped. I was lucky I didn't have a visit from a few Def Jam brothers to rough me up that night.

In the end, let the record show that the winner of *America's Next Top Model* was *not* my choice. I take an aesthetic view of beauty and perfection. This image has been etched in my mind since I was nine years old, poring over the pages of *Vogue* at my local supermarket. I believe a model should be lean, healthy, and toned.

"What are you talking about?" I said. "You're crazy! She's perfect." But I knew my definition of beauty wasn't politically correct. It's not that I didn't *like* the winner—I did—or that I thought she couldn't have a future in the business. It's just that there was a better choice.

But what really cracked me up was what the winner said after she got the title. "God, this has been a great experience—because more than anything I love Janice Dickinson," she said. "Just meeting her has changed my life."

"Don't love me," I told her. "I didn't vote for you."

But she remained true to herself—and insisted I'd told her things she'd take with her forever.

Maybe she has some potential after all.

8.
How I Feel About the Modeling World Now

Bottom line: I *adore* models. I think we deserve our own planet, a Model World with soft lighting twenty-four hours a day and full-length mirrors on every corner. In Model World, McDonald's and Burger King would be replaced with drive-thru veggie stands, and free moisturizer would come at the end of dinner instead of free mints. Every bedsheet would be 300-count-plus; every meal would be low-fat; every sunny day would begin with a hot cabana boy showing up at your casa with a bottle of personally calibrated sunscreen and a smile. President Dolce and VP Gabbana would only lead their nation to war over the really serious issues—like ensuring adequate supplies of high-quality foreign leather for Manolo Blahnik's new fall line.

Sure, I've been through a hell of a lot with my model friends: the competition, the rivalry, the backbiting, and the blow jobs. But I don't hate my sisters. Hate is such a strong word—plus it gives you worry lines.

I prefer to think of us all living in harmony in Model World—sharing our best beauty secrets all week long, then pausing on Sunday to pray for our souls . . . and a permanent form of Botox.

If you know me at all, you may think that's all a load of bull. But let me just say this: just because you have an attitude doesn't mean you're hateful.

Back in the late 1970s, I was up for a Bloomingdales shoot. It was a huge cattle call of beautiful faces, and I entered a room filled with about a hundred models, all of us waiting to charm a famed lingerie photographer. Naturally, the Big Dog didn't wait her turn in the back of the room; I just bumped those toned asses aside and pushed my way to the front of the line.

Was this mean? Was this hateful? *Nah.* Photographer Guy Bourdin loved my sense of superiority and hired me on the spot. He knew I'd earned my sense of entitlement.

The sad truth is, there'll always be rivalry among women—whether we're talking models or housewives or business execs. Sit any two women at a table and they'll be eyeballing each other to death in no time. Life is a reality show—just like *America's Next Top Model.*

There's a famous photo of Sophia Loren eyeballing Jayne Mansfield's breasts at a dinner party in the 1960s. Even though she's always had one of the world's most beautiful figures in the world—hell, she still *does*— poor Sophia has a look of astonishment on her face. Why? Because she knows no one could beat Jayne's tits. I don't care how much Italian food Sophia ate, them thar hills on her chest weren't about to grow another cup size. There were two choices: shove Jayne out of her chair, or live with it.

Luckily, Sophia isn't a violent woman.

Opposite: Self-portrait. False eyelashes, push-up bras, and heels for day. Studio in Hollywood, California, 1990.

When it comes to rivalry, though, I know we models' cups runneth over. So I'm experimenting with a new telephone hotline service I created called Models Anonymous. I opened the line earlier this year—and, basically, now I've got models calling me day and night to report in about their feelings of jealousy and betrayal. I just listen to these angst-ridden beauties tell their tales of woe, and throw 'em whatever pearls of wisdom I can.

Last night, for instance, one famous model called. "Janice, I'm still fighting that sugar doughnut problem." In the old days, if I ran across a model with a white streak beneath her nostrils, I'd be pretty comfortable betting it was cocaine. Now—with this girl, anyway—it's more likely to be powdered sugar.

"You have to wean yourself off," I responded. "Can't you just make toast and put a little Equal on it? Trick your mind." *Click.* Another life saved.

**Kim Charlton and Jerry Hall primping before a shoot.
A whole lot of work goes into the preparation.**

Other well-known models have called me to talk about perverted photographers, nasty agents who withhold commissions, bulimia, anorexia, jealous boyfriends—the works. They report in on a daily basis, and together we mull over the dark side of the biz. I'm there to listen. I've even thought about writing a standard set of twelve steps to help get models over the rough spots:

STEP #1: Admit that you're a model, and that you're powerless over makeup and hair care products.

STEP #2: Estée Lauder is our leader. Bow to her every morning.

I won't take this too far—I take my AA program too seriously to make fun of something that saved my life—but you get the idea.

But I can understand why these girls need something—some kind of understanding voice. If I pieced together all the magazine layouts and ads I've done in my lifetime, the paper trail would go for miles; it certainly took me around the world. And after twenty-five years in this business, I'm *still* not satisfied with the way I look. I can find serenity sometimes if I'm wearing a beautiful black cocktail dress with some dope evening shoes. Once, when I really needed to make myself feel better, I went to a coffee shop dressed that way, without a camera around me. Today I don't just dress for the designers or the photographers. I dress for *myself*.

Every so often, though, it's not just about me. Which brings us to the next part of this book, which I like to call "The Circle of (Social) Life."

I'm not talking about the Disney song, but my very own definition of the circle of life: dating, marriage, drinking, divorce, remarriage, more drinking, more divorce, a little whoring around, a little more drinking . . .

At least that's how it was back in the day.

PART II
THE CIRCLE OF (SOCIAL) LIFE

Before I continue, let me address the number-one question I'm asked these days by friends, fans, and foes. It goes a little something like this: "So, Janice, I loved the first book. But didn't any of the celebrities you mentioned get a little *upset* with you for relaying the intimate details of the time you spent totally naked and horizontal with them?"

My response: "You mean who's called me to say they're pissed? No one. Bottom line: those guys were lucky they made the cut."

I believe in kissing and telling; I figure I've earned the right. We're talking about my *memoirs*, for God's sake. These A-list actors should all chill out; I was famous before many of them were—and, whether they like it or not, they know that everything I said about them (flattering or not) was true.

And the same goes for what you're about to read. Everything I'm about to tell you actually happened. Every playboy, every shah or sultan, every movie star or rock 'n' roll star, woke up at some point in his life and realized he wanted me. And many of them still do.

When it comes to sex, I think we're all animals. We like to fuck. You can put us in nice clothes that cost a mint and take us out to watch

Shakespeare in the Park, but we still can't wait to get home and rip off each other's threads. Admit it: how many times have you been on a date to some boring event, thinking only one thought: *Am I going to get laid tonight or not?* Life is about sex. Shakespeare knew it: what were Romeo and Juliet, after all, but a couple of horny teenagers? You *know* Beethoven liked sex—and that was in the days before deodorant.

Now, I know you're dying to hear some more stories about the men in my life. Before we get to the current boldface names, though, let's take a quick trek to the past, which is where I got all screwed up about men in the first place . . .

9.
My Teenage Wasteland

Where did I become obsessed with perfection? Back in the badlands of Florida, where the insecurity juggernaut began to take shape when I was just a teenager. The minute I hit puberty, it hit back—hard.

I was the latest bloomer on my block—or any block in America, for that matter. At the age of fifteen I was still an ironing board with legs. I was tall and dark, with no curves, no nothing, and I took heat for it from everyone around me. Life was all about surface, and mine was completely flat. I wasn't the girl in *Seventeen* magazine with the long, flowing blonde hair and big blue eyes. Instead, I was a duckling who was sure that swanhood would never come.

From my Rat Bastard dad on down, I left my childhood feeling damaged and extremely needy. So in my teen years I went looking for answers anywhere I could, knowing that all this angst wasn't good for my brain. (Or my skin, for that matter.) I tried to do the standard chick thing, which was to enroll in ballet class. But the teacher took one look in my direction and decided her only move was to demolish me.

"Are you serious about ballet?" she asked. In response, I took four classes a week to please her.

One day, she went into her patented tenth position, which involved pinching her mouth into the ugliest sneer ever.

"*Janeeece!*" she barked as I struggled to follow her. "Why are we even bothering? You're much too tall to ever become a dancer." This coming from an old spinster drone who was much too ugly to do anything but dash the dreams of young girls.

So I switched ballet classes. My new teacher was a big fat slob, a one-time thin dancer who got married and took up smoking and Dunkin' Donuts. "I'm just not feeling your passion," she'd sneer at me between mouthfuls of creamy custard and sugary dough.

I was certainly feeling her calories. How could she eat all those cheap fast-food carbs in front of me while I was trying to dance my heart out, starving for the Broadway stage? Hooray for Hollywood (Florida), I thought to myself. Here's a woman who fancies herself a ballerina, when she knows her best move is leaping to the fridge in the middle of the night—face-first.

Fat Fattie also borrowed a little trick from my old friends the storm trooper nuns: she'd take a ruler out of her desk and "tap" us girls to make us inch up higher on our developing teenage toes. One too many taps, and I chucked it all for an early retirement from a life in ballet. I just couldn't take the bruises, or the bullshit.

My father had wanted a boy, as he never failed to remind me. So for a while I thought I'd give him the next best thing and behave like one. That's why the world's first supermodel spent her early years trying to get to first base—literally—as a member of the boys' high school baseball team. It wasn't the kind of diamond Marilyn Monroe had cooed about, but I was hell-bent on proving to myself that girls can kick boys' asses (I'm still working on that one). Back then, though, it wasn't that hard: to put it politely (or as nicely as I possibly can), it was tenth grade and Janice was the only one on the team with any balls.

As usual, men have a way of trying to psych a strong woman out.

"Aim for her tits," said the baseball coach during the endless practices every day after school. "Her chest! *Her chest!*"

Prick. Needless to say, he wasn't thrilled with the idea of affirmative action, which had put someone with a vagina on his team. There wasn't a damn thing he could do about it—except take an already awkward situation and make it worse.

Part of the problem was that he didn't like the press, who came out in droves to interview me for the community news section of the local rag. It was my first brush with fame, and I loved being the girl who ran with the boys. Unfortunately for me, though, my teammates were good at taking orders from their coach. In the end, my blossoming, aching breasts just couldn't take any more fastballs aimed right at my nipples.

I don't want you to think I'm a quitter. I stayed on the team as long as humanly possible. But before the season was over, I realized I'd had it with huge, ugly bruises.

"Fuck, I get enough abuse at home. Who needs this shit?" I finally told the coach, peeling off my jersey and throwing it at his feet. (Don't worry, I had a tank top on underneath.)

He noticed that I was still holding the ball. "Janice," he said, "that's school property. You can't take anything home as a souvenir for your time running with the big boys."

I wound up and gave him my best fastball—which landed squarely in his nuts.

"Oh, my God," I said, smiling. "Fly ball!"

It was a perfect moment, one of the very few of my teenage years.

With my Major League career down the tubes, I had to focus on how to use my newfound sports knowledge for an even more important pursuit: men. At night, I'd pore over old movie magazines and dream about getting to second base with Cary Grant, Gregory Peck, Spencer Tracy, and Sidney Poitier—although I think the members of my little Florida community would have dropped dead if they'd seen one of their own little white chicks dating Mr. Tibbs. Ebony and ivory was only for Oreo cookies and the keys on the piano at school.

When I wasn't obsessing about boys, I joined the school band. I had to do something to entertain myself, but there were problems from the start. My ultrabig lips didn't mesh with that tiny trumpet mouthpiece, and I didn't make first seat. Pissed off—and sick of the constant dry mouth—I quit the band . . . and decided to put those lips to a better use.

At first, I was hardly able to envision myself as worthy of a real boyfriend. So I spent my free time dreaming of living in another era, when the leading men of the silver screen would find their way to Florida, take one look at the skinny, small-chested girl with the good pitching arm, and say, "Why, it's love. Come away with me, Janice, to Hollywood, California! You can sit on a chair by a pool, where servants will bring you chilled grapes and peel them for you, too."

I didn't even *like* grapes. But that image was imbedded in my mind. I devoured every old movie I found on TV; they all featured men who acted like real men—and most of them could dance! Unlike most of the boys in my school, they'd heard of simple things like a bar of soap. Clark Gable knew about hair gel before it cost thirty bucks.

No wonder the local boys weren't flocking to my screen door. Somehow I thought having stick-straight hair like Cher might help, but back in the day we didn't have flatirons. I ironed my hair with . . . yes, the vacuum cleaner.

When no one was looking I'd get out a nice, white towel, carefully unroll my waist-length hair on it, then take the bottom part of our huge Hoover and run it over my locks—until I smelled that horrid hairburning smell, which was my signal to turn it off. It was a little gross, but it worked. (Especially after I learned how to rig the vacuum cleaner to keep the exhaust from pouring in my face, which did my pores no good).

In my quest to look like a young babe, I paid careful attention to learning how to put on makeup. My mother didn't realize it, but her daughter Janice had her under constant surveillance. With the intensity of an FBI agent-in-training, I'd zero in on Mom as she put on her makeup in our old Buick. She applied that glossy tube of Revlon scarlet lipstick

($1.99 at the local drugstore) with the precision of any great dame who was about to go out in the world and be noticed. I took it all in, keeping mental notes on how to go a little above and below her lip line for the perfect sexy pout.

At sixteen, I called my private beauty studies to a close and prepared to go public. That's when I discovered the beach, which was an entirely new world for me. Florida was full of girls who practically lived on the beach—who preferred sand between their toes to wall-to-wall shag carpeting. Unlike me, however, most of them had that one unmistakable sign of female perfection going for them: they were blonde.

With my dark hair, I stood out like the subject of one of those *Sesame Street* skits: "One of these things is not like the other."

Before John Frieda ever came up with products that make you impossibly blonder, I would spy on the beach girls, who would get their little pump cans out of their bags and "put sun" into their hair with lemon juice and salt water.

Knowing that I didn't have the right skin type (mine's olive) or eye color (baby browns) to fake being a blonde, I skipped the hair harem's advice and decided to perfect my tan. Back then, no one really worried about little things like skin cancer or wrinkles. We just sat out there with our big bottles of baby oil (oooh, how I love that smell). We even dropped some iodine in there now and then, just to add some sizzle.

I wasn't kidding: it was the 1960s, and I was shooting for the same skin tone as Diana Ross (Miss Ross to you and me). But that wasn't exactly happening: I was shooting for black, but I ended up red, burned, and peeling. In desperation, I even pulled out one of those fabulous aluminum tanning shields that made George Hamilton the leathery-looking senior citizen he is today.

"Fry, bitch, fry," I'd tell myself.

In many ways, I think this was my very first addiction. It's amazing that I didn't just fry up into a little nub and get washed away by the ocean. I guess my motto—*only the strong survive*—holds true even when it comes to nature's wrath on the body.

With all this bathing suit and tanning action going on, you might assume I was also sneaking under the boardwalk for a little harmless afternoon delight with the local boys. That wasn't necessarily the case: thanks to my father, sex was my version of the late-night horror show.

Drugs were another matter. Timothy Leary could have used me as an example of living on the edge. I discovered drugs at my friend Eric's house. At thirteen, I'd go over to his house to get stoned on pot, which led to

Trying to strike a pose.

some great bouts of shoplifting. I'd steal some records, and we'd go back to Eric's house to drink, get high, blast the music, and dance.

Later on, my friends Maria and Jill and I would go to the beach, sip some beers, and wait for our LSD to kick in. All I ever did when I was that high was think of The Monster (a.k.a. my father), though, and that wasn't a good feeling. I knew it was just the drugs, but I didn't want to go there.

The problem was, I couldn't avoid the drug scene. One day, one of my guy friends, who was a dealer of sorts, asked me to check out his stolen Volkswagen.

"Hey, Janice, get a load of what's in the backseat," said Rick. Glancing back there, I saw what looked like baby powder, all packaged up in little plastic Baggies. It was unbelievable: Rick had rolls and rolls of acid in those baggies, most of them stuffed under this sand-filled flannel blanket he kept in the hatchback. Back then everyone seemed to be doing acid and pot.

"Do you want to get high?" he asked me. Until then, to tell the truth, I'd never really been in love with pot—I hated the smell of it. But Rick's car reeked of really good Jamaican gold; Rick himself was supercute; and I was only too happy to sit on the front of the car with him, listen to the waves crash, do acid, and sing along to Pink Floyd on his radio.

The only problem was, when I was high I'd lose track of time. Watching the sunrise with Rick that night, I knew a new day was about to begin—along with a new load of shit when I got home.

"Fuck! Rick, you've gotta drive me home," I told him, and made him drop me off about a block away. When we got close to my street, I vaulted out of the VW and snuck around the bushes until I saw my house. *Please, let them all be asleep*, I prayed. If I was lucky, I'd turn the doorknob and no one would stir. (Among other things, I really needed the peace and quiet—I was still tripping hard.)

That night, like plenty of others, I was lucky. I came downstairs about six hours later, trying to appear normal. "Is it Saturday or Sunday?" I asked my little sister, Debbie, a blond, blue-eyed junior gymnast. By this time, my older sister, Alexis, had moved out. Debbie just rolled her eyes.

The good news was, my parents' lack of interest in my life was actually working in my favor. My mother, a nurse, was busy experimenting with her own bottles of pills; she was too out of it to care. My father was always prowling around somewhere; not seeing him was a blessing.

I liked the drugs because they kept me in this perfect fantasy life that I couldn't find when I was straight. As a teenager, my own private Shangri-la was a pretty swinging place; my mind was always on overdrive. When I retreated into this fantasyland, it was only Janice and her black science teacher, Mr. Curtis, with the hot, bulging arm muscles.

Sure, I almost failed science. But that's just because my mind was pre-occupied with a different kind of chemistry.

Back on the beach, my hormones finally reached the boiling point: something had to happen, and soon. That's when I set my pubescent sights on Vincent "Vinnie" Scurra, a hot surfer dude with curly blond hair and a bod that made him look like an outdoorsy Sonny Corleone. A very outgoing Italian, my Vinnie had this way of making girls melt—no silver tanning shield required. Every single time he'd catch a wave, he'd sing a chorus of the Beatles' "Get Back," and my knees would go weak. Inside, I was quaking: not only did Vinnie move with the swiftness of a fawn, he was *nice* to me!

Eventually, though, it became apparent that Vinny was being friendly not because he wanted to get into my bikini bottoms. No, he had the worst ulterior motive of all: *he actually wanted to be friends.* I was just "one of the guys," Vinnie told me; I couldn't get into his "girls' club."

"Honey, you're not blonde," he said. "You don't even have tits. You're like a little sister to me." He got a mascot for himself and his other guy friends; all I got was a big hug that left me (alone) feeling hot.

"Do you think Samantha likes me?" Vinnie asked, pointing to one of the girls on the beach who would spend her days twirling her long blonde locks and adjusting her big tits, and her nights giving out BJs under the boardwalk.

"She likes *everyone*," I replied. "Plus, check out her fat thighs." (That line comes in handy: I used it again years later on a runway in Paris.)

"You think she's fat?" Vinnie gasped; he actually sounded concerned. I know it was nasty, but I had to clear the deck when it came to competition—or at least try.

I also put the word out on Sheila, this white-bread, curvy number. Sheila was pretty popular—until the rumor started going around that she was suffering from something awful that made her itch in places you didn't want to be scratching. Yep, this was my way of covering the hurt: if I wasn't good enough for Vinnie, then I might as well put a verbal hit on the girls who were.

I was in total pain and anguish in those days because I simply didn't fit in at all. I wasn't a good student; my home life sucked; even at the beach where I came to belong, I was on the outside looking in.

At age sixteen, I decided there was only one solution: I would become the perfect all-American teenager. My first step was to rejoin the band, but when I failed to take first seat once again—this time with my new love, the clarinet—I was miserable. I practiced like a bitch; didn't practice make perfect at this fucked-up school? Obviously not! I even ran for student council, but who was going to vote for weird Janice?

In my spare time, of course, I practically lived on the cold tile of the local Publix supermarket, poring over all the girls in the magazines. That's where I assembled my little pantheon of heroines: Lauren Hutton in Halston, Marisa Berenson in Coco Chanel, Catherine Deneuve in a St. Laurent tuxedo. I saved up the few dollars I earned working at the pizza parlor to buy the latest fashion mags. It got to the point where Doris, the checker at Publix, would call me to let me know when the latest issue of *Vogue* was in.

My obsession with modeling must have been pretty all-encompassing: eventually even my mother snapped to it enough to take a day off from work to drive me to an audition at the John Robert Powers School of Modeling. "You're a beautiful girl," my mother told me, and just hearing the words made me want to cry. But Dawn Nichols, the tough-looking chick who ran the school, took one look at my raisinlike breasts, visible ribs, and long, nondescript hair, asked my mother to write out a check, and stepped into her new role as Janice's Latest Tormentor.

The next day, I returned for my first modeling lesson: How to Walk Properly. It seemed to go well, but Dawn made one thing perfectly clear to me: "You'll never make it as" —*snicker, snort*— "a *model*. You don't really have a body, dear. You look like . . . well, a boy."

"Maybe I could be a boy model," I snapped back.

"Dear, I don't need your sarcasm."

"You haven't *met* my sarcasm yet," I hissed. She just turned away, trying to stick to her lessons about walking around with a phone book on your head.

The whole modeling school experience only added one more layer of pain to my life. *Everyone* told me I wasn't worthy, over and over, until I heard their voices in my sleep. As we all know, sometimes it's hard to get rid of those little voices. When everyone is telling you that you're not perfect and never will be, it seeps into every corner of your sorrowful soul.

Only later did I discover what it takes—a lot of real work, and plenty of struggle—to get those voices to fuck off.

By the age of seventeen, I was starting to get a feeling for where my true salvation would come from: the gorgeous rock 'n' roll of Jim Morrison (my hero), and my prized handful of low-priced G-string bathing suits, which were finally helping me catch the eyes of a few guys on the beach. I was the original Frankie B. Girl, mostly because I was so broke. My wardrobe at the time consisted of rock T-shirts from concerts (like my favorite shredded Jimi Hendrix one), a battered leather jacket, and lowrise, landlubber jeans. Way before these teeny pop-tart stars today "invented" that look, I pioneered it.

Opposite: If in doubt, sing as loud as you possibly can. The energy will come through.

Unfortunately, the people of South Florida didn't give a rat's ass about fashion. I was still treating the magazine rack at Publix like a library, even though the meanest checker there loved giving me shit for my studies. "You have to *buy* the magazine if you want to read it," she'd inform me, then walk her fat ass away to the back of the store for yet another dough-nut break. I just handed her the magazine and told her, "Read and learn." Still, it was hard trying to convince people in my town that poly-ester wasn't the official national fabric.

In my quest to be dazzling, I caused a major shakeup at my own se-nior prom. I went to the big occasion with my boyfriend, Bobby McCarthy, a cute little stud with dark brown eyes and actual chest hair. Imagine the looks on everyone's prudish faces when I, Janice, walked into the prom wearing a pair of elephant-legged silver lamé disco pants I'd seen in *Vogue* and used half a year's savings to buy through the mail. Everything was silver, from my skintight silver silk shirt to my sparkling eye shadow and stiletto pumps. Unfortunately, I was also pretty stoned, and I was too 'luded out to register the reactions of my beloved classmates and teachers.

Standing there with me in his rented black tux, Bobby reminded me that we'd enjoyed ourselves much more at the recent Doors concert. Maybe we ought to get back in the car, put on a Doors tape, and just fool around like we had been doing for the past several months.

He was right. Even back then I knew that the most important thing af-ter making a big entrance was not to overstay your welcome. Bobby and I hit the road after about fifteen minutes, and soon all that silver lamé was in a heap on the floor of his Mustang.

So what does it all mean?

I think there's no perfect way to end your childhood—and that's why the ultramessy teen years were created. Teenage girls are basically screwed from the get-go: you're entering young womanhood, your hor-mones are doing strange things to your body, and you're a prime target for all sorts of men just drooling to bone a sweet young thing. And don't even try looking inward because all you'll find is turmoil! Here we go again . . . all you want is to be perfect, but everyone from your family to your teachers insists on reminding you that you're far from it.

Now, more than ever, society is putting increased emphasis on looking perfect. Everything's retouched, except what hurts us deep inside. The other day I met a sixteen-year-old girl who told me she wanted to buy a set of boobs like the ones I have because she *absolutely needed* to look like the women she saw on the pages of magazines. "Janice, I've smooshed my boobs into all those Victoria's Secret push-up bras," she cried. "It still isn't enough."

I tried to tell her that the girls in the magazines only look that way after surgery, followed by two and a half hours in a makeup chair, followed by a nice hot session of Photoshop. "Do you honestly have the budget and the time to try all that before going to first period English class?" I asked. She admitted I had a point.

Young girls, I beg you: listen to me for two seconds here. When you see someone in a magazine or on TV, remember: it's all a big façade. Those models you see on the pages of *Seventeen* and *Elle* starve themselves for weeks on end, smoke up a storm, scarf down diuretics, and then, when everyone's still unhappy with their photos, someone sits at a computer and points-and-clicks them into Perfect, Unreal Sexiness.

I really believe that what's going on in the pages of magazines is scarring the young women of today. I know it must be hard for them—because it was murder for girls like me back in the 1960s, well before the first horny little computer magician ever enhanced the size of a girl's cleavage. Hell, I may have been the world's first supermodel, but my youth was just as fucked up as anyone else's.

Maybe if my parents had been more stable (or at least more blond), I might have had a shot. From the start, nothing in my life was even close to decent, let alone perfect—with the possible exception of those silver lamé pants.

And it didn't get any easier as I got older, let me tell you. My dealings with men only drove me further and further away from that perfect little happily-ever-after dream we're all force-fed from childhood.

10.

Men, Age, and Perfection

As you get closer to perfection nirvana, I've found, it's harder to keep men under control. Frankly, the male of the species doesn't know what to do with a woman who has it pretty much together; in his struggle to keep up, you'll find he often reverts to his five-year-old self.

One night in the mid-1980s, I was at Mezzaluna in Los Angeles with a soon-to-be ex-boyfriend (who shall remain nameless, poor guy). Just as my date walked away to get our drinks, actor and former model Jack Scalia approached me. Frankly, I don't know how it happened, but suddenly Jack was kissing me.

After I pried his lips off mine, I appealed to his common sense. "Jack," I said. "This is a modeling-industry party. Please, be the poster boy for manners." Two seconds later, we were making out again—this time for real. (Jack is a great kisser; what could I do?) That's when things got a little ugly. My date came back, slammed his two cranberry cocktails on the table, and with one of his newly free hands made a fist and took a hard swing at Jack.

I guess all those Lifetime cable movies paid off for Jack: he really knew how to duck and move. As I was reapplying my lip gloss, I screamed: "Can you please stop acting like children! I don't really like either one of you that much anyway. And this is *way* too much drama for everyone."

Suddenly the fists stopped flying—and soon Jack and my date were trading notes on why "women are such bitches."

This was my cue to leave. I hit the dance floor, grabbed the nearest eighteen-year-old Calvin Klein protégé, and danced his ass off. He couldn't handle it, either, and slinked away after two songs.

Stories like this have always made me wonder if there really *is* a perfect man out there for me . . . or anyone else, for that matter. In the interest of social science, I've conducted my own experiments over the years, looking for the perfect species of man.

Allow me to share some of the results of my research . . .

Younger Men

I went on this date about six months ago with a bunch of friends—but what a bunch. It was like Romper Room, with yours truly as chaperone. The crowd included Kim Stewart (Rod's daughter), Jack Osbourne (son of Sharon and Ozzy), and Orbie Orbison, son of the legendary Roy. Clearly, no one in the room had as many miles on the odometer as I did—but who's counting?

As we sat there in Rod Stewart's guesthouse waiting for the evening to get started, I wasn't exactly in a partying mood. To be honest, I was feeling like the Jurassic supermodel. Still, instead of wallowing in my own private pity party, I looked around the room and noticed something odd—in the form of a spark between Orbie and myself.

Yikes! I thought. *He's so much younger. Then again, what the hell?*

"Hey, everybody," I announced, still thinking through the possibilities. "Why are we just sitting around like this? I thought we were going to go out and dance. Or is this just going to be another wasted evening?"

A few minutes later our limo was pulling up to A.D., a hot club in North Hollywood.

By the time we got out I was holding hands with Orbie. In my head all I could hear was his father singing. Well, I *was* a pretty woman that night, in my red Diane von Furstenberg fuck-me wrap dress with matching dolly-dagger let's-get-it-on Blahnik disco shoes. As soon as we entered the club, I noticed what looked like a bunch of Pablo Escobar wannabes to my right; on my left, Jack Osbourne was signing an autograph. Soon my twenty-eight-year-old "date," Orbie, was putting back tequila shooters. I could tell the whole thing was freaking him out.

Just holding hands with a woman old enough to be his "teacher" (to put it politely, which I don't usually like to do) was enough to send him into a massive anxiety attack. Soon he was shitfaced enough to start speaking his mind. "You're hot," he shouted. "You're hotter than those girls in the corner. You're hotter than Julia Roberts!" (I took that as a compliment.)

After a few minutes on the dance floor, a beer bottle whizzed past my head, and I ducked just in time to hear Jack tell some faceless detractor to fuck off. Then a second bottle came flying, but this one caught Orbie's nose, which ended up looking sort of broken.

Oh, brother, I thought. *Younger men—it* sounds *like a good idea, but do I really need the beer 'n' fistfights?* I just hoped no one would puke on my new shoes; I didn't think my leather cleaner could handle it.

Before long we were all piling into a chaperoned SUV that had just pulled up, with Rod's personal driver behind the wheel. (Rod didn't want his daughter partying without his driver there for a little extra protection.) In the backseat I nursed Orbie's nose; the blood soaked through big wads of Kleenex.

"Maybe we should go to the hospital," I suggested. He just shook his head—*out of the question.*

"I want you to go home with me and make me feel better," he implored me. Well, I did have a little crush on the kid. So, yes, I went home with him, and, yes, I made him feel better.

Why? Because he was so cute? Because he had such a hard bod? Because he was Roy Orbison's son?

Would you accept "just because"?

So what's the perfect age when it comes to dating? I don't really care about a number on a driver's license, and frankly most men don't seem to care about my age, either. Once you hit the supermodel level, your numerical time spent on Earth doesn't matter to men. They're not fucking Mrs. Robinson, they're fucking a supermodel. If I were a dental hygienist or worked behind the counter at Avis, I doubt I'd get the same play.

Come hither, ye ole farm boys!

For me, younger guys have two things going for them: they certainly have stamina, and they don't like to get too deep when it comes to a woman's psyche.

A few years ago, when I was living in Southampton, New York, I once *accidentally* threw my very toned, mile-long leg over one of my neighbors' son. Call it a reflex; maybe my leg just slipped due to an excess of suntan lotion. It wasn't my fault that this kid was six feet tall, bronzed, dark-haired, blue-eyed—your basic garden-variety Adonis. Oh, he was also eighteen. The only problem was, once he whipped off his Ray Bans, the first words out of his mouth weren't exactly the stuff of great romantics.

"So, like, you were really on the cover of *Cosmo?*" he said. "That's awesome!" Then he made some finger sign that I hoped didn't mean he believed in devil worship.

An hour later we went upstairs, and *he was, like, pounding a* Cosmo *cover girl.* The sex was fine, but that day I *did* feel a little Mrs. Robinson. Trust me, no one wants to feel that much "older" while in the sack.

There are a few other disadvantages to slumming with the kids. "Do you ever wash these sheets?" I asked after we were done.

"My mom says the same thing," he griped. Two seconds later I was out of there.

In defense of younger men, I like to smell their innocence; I revel in their inexperience. It's perfectly good fun to be the teacher now and then, and most of these little stud puppies are so damn grateful for the lesson.

Oh, and in case you're a young man reading this book, let me toss you some good advice: Don't be intimidated. Janice grades on a curve.

Sometimes life throws you some interesting curves, which is how I hooked up with freshly minted action icon Vin Diesel and young, adorable rock star Justin Timberlake.

Let me preface this by saying that young boys just give me *energy*. It's like being jacked up on speed, and since I don't take drugs anymore, this is the next best thing. This is why lately I've made it my business on Saturday nights to go clubbing at all the hot spots on Sunset Boulevard.

A few weeks ago, I was shaking my still-thin groove thing when this hot baldie came up to give me a whirl.

"Hi, I'm Vin," said Mr. Diesel. As if I couldn't have figured it out for myself. I can't even count how many times my son, Nathan, has rented *The Fast and the Furious*.

"I know you are. I love this song. Dance with me if you want to talk," I yelled. He stayed and we swayed, toned hip to $20-million-a-movie hip.

A few seconds later, I whipped my head around when a blur of streaked blond hair caught my eye. (Sorry, Vin, but even in your presence, this ass demanded my attention.)

This youngun had moves to spare—and he looked sort of familiar. Then it dawned on me. Man, oh, man, that Britney Spears made a huge mistake.

Talk about an adrenalin rush. Suddenly I was the meat in a superstar sandwich. Vin and Justin were dancing around me, and every single woman in the place looked as if she wanted to shoot me dead.

What did these girls expect? I'd put in the hours. I'd been working on my clubbing look for weeks, checking out what the sistas were doing when it came to Saturday-night shake-your-ass fashion. I've always loved how so many black chicks wear whatever they want, and I envy them for it. Women of all shapes and sizes in this culture love to go out on the town in body-hugging white tank tops, a great bra, and a microminiskirt made out of fibers that hug everything and anything. Out on the dance floor, the need to be perfect loses way to sweating like a pig and letting go.

It's good advice for life: just dance, dance, dance, and don't stop. That sort of freedom is fabulous—it's also perfectly acceptable.

As for Justin, he was an adorable, sweet, and caring boy. Vin, on the other hand, was a little too *stanky* for Janice. Hey, Vin, a little suggestion from your dance partner: you ought to dish out some of that $20 mil on a stick of deodorant. Not to mention, I'm not into shiny scalps. I just don't find them all that sexy—on most guys, anyway. The only sexy guy who can rock the look is Bruce Willis (stay tuned—more on him later). Then again, I also dig Michael Chiklis from that new, hot, dirty cop show *The*

Shield. (Girls, get over your crushes on him. He's happily married and loves his wife. Even sexier!) I met him once in yoga class while he was getting his body in shape, and the guy has never seemed happier. I wonder if his wife would mind loaning him out for a little Saturday-night dancing . . .

Sean Connery, This Means You

Now, let's flip the switch and talk about that oh-so-Hollywood trend: old geezers hooking up with young babes like myself. Compared to some of these older movie stars, well, I could be their great-granddaughter. (Of course, I wouldn't mind playing that role—in exchange for a nice trust fund and a summer home.)

When it comes to sex, my general reaction is: "Older guys?! Yuck." Ask a woman who knows: when you're walking on the beach in St. Barts, you're not looking for some wrinkly old dude, but a young, strapping stud. To quote my ex, Sylvester Stallone: "When you wander into the pet shop, you don't leave with the old dog. You go home with the puppy." Ah, Sly, you always were so poetic.

I have made a few exceptions, of course. When I've dated much older men, I've found that it bothered them more than me. Age never really bothers me that much in the men I date—because I always choose the pick of the litter.

I had a major love jones for Peter Beard. He was much older than *moi*, but it didn't matter because he was the hottest guy on the planet. When I saw him running around in nothing but his sandals, it really turned me on. There were no creases anywhere that didn't belong there. And there's something sexy about any man who can tell you how he once was mauled by a bull elephant—and show you the scars to prove it. My only complaint? His feet were awfully rough from all that walking barefoot around the Serengeti, wearing nothing but his legendary good looks.

What's a girl to do when such a warrior says to you, "Hey, Janny, come up to my hotel room?" Well, I thought about it—but believe it or not, I didn't go. At the time he was married to a good friend of mine. If that hadn't been the case, I would have hopped between those sheets in a New York minute, even though he was old enough to be my uncle.

When it comes to age and sex, when you meet your match, the numbers don't matter. When the arrows of Cupid hit their marks, who gives a rat's ass how many years you've both spent on the planet?

Now that we've covered some of the perks of dating men—young and old—let's get real and have a look at how men can fuck up even the most perfect relationships.

It's not just their job—it's their pleasure.

11.

My School of Discipline

The other day, a fellow feline pulled up a latte next to mine and asked me the century-old question, "Can you change a man?"

My response? "*Abso-fucking-lutely*. Pass me an Equal and I'll explain all."

This was a subject I could warm to. "Honey, let me make one thing perfectly clear," I told her. "If you want to change a guy, you've got to enroll him in an institution that's more respected than Harvard, tougher to graduate from than Yale, and certainly more magical than that joint where Harry Potter learned his moves." The institution of female higher learning I'm talking about is called My School of Discipline (MSD). And I'm accepting applications.

As the dean and founder of MSD, I can say that the courses are tough, the instructor *(moi)* no-nonsense. But those who graduate have a 100 percent success rate in the real world of male/female bullshit. I don't charge tuition; the knowledge I've gained from being married three times, and then being thrust back out into the dating world afterward, is so important that I feel it must be passed on to the masses. It's the least I can do—and it helps me even the score with any man out there who might have dissed me in the past. (You know who you are, Mick.)

So grab your pad and pen and get ready to take notes because school's in session. My name is Ms. Dickinson, and I'm ready to teach you everything you need to know in order to beat men at their own game.

First things first: why do you need to enter MSD? Because, ladies, when a dog shits in the house, you've got to rub his face in it if he's ever going to learn not to do it again. If you don't rub your man's face in the emotional shit he dishes out, trust me—he'll just pull *the same* garbage, over and over again.

The fact is, I think it's best to treat most men like they're pets. If they don't meet your expectations, they need to be put outside—in the doghouse. Lesson number one: Don't call or e-mail him when he's in the doghouse. (Technology has done us no favors in this area, if you ask me.)

Men will screw up, and they must be punished—that is, if you're trying to have a reasonable relationship. If you want to continue being tormented by men, by all means, stop reading and go back to your regularly scheduled life.

Even in the best of times, you've got to practice your lessons in discipline. For instance, one weekend I had a great sexathon with my now-former flame. Think I called him the next morning to invite him over for a recap? Forget it. I didn't call him for three days. And it's not that I was being a bitch. It's all about taking the power back. He had a lot of power during our two days in bed, and I walked out of his bedroom with a smile on my face. But life has given me the know-how to recognize when it's time to snap out of a sex haze and reclaim my position as Big Dog.

Instead, I spent the next day or so on the phone with my girlfriends while he just sat at home wondering, *Why isn't she calling? Should I call her? Maybe she's mad at me. Maybe I'm not that great after all . . .* I burned off a few calories working out and writing, and managed to keep my mind off how much I wanted to pick up that phone and pour out words of adoration to My Man of the Hour. As we all know, that can be the worst possible move of all.

Did he deserve the silent treatment? Let's look at the record. In the beginning, we would talk for hours on the phone. Long-distance love—ain't it a bitch? In the weeks before the sexathon, however, our telephone exchanges had dwindled down to fifteen-minute conversations, and I wasn't happy about it.

Here's my guarantee to you: after a few days of no contact, most boyfriends will come up with plenty of new things to talk about.

Take the power back. You'll lose that coveted spark unless you take back the remote control of the relationship.

Three days later, of course, he finally broke down and called me. I talked for exactly five minutes before I checked my watch and told him, "Okay—gotta go." It was a very abrupt ending, and I knew the question marks were flying through his brain. As predicted, he called me back that night to see if I was doing okay. Again, I made it nice and quick: "Really can't talk right now," I said cheerfully, and put down the receiver.

The next morning he rang up again, just to say hello and wish me a perfect day. It was a wonderful way to start the day—with my man acting the way I wanted him to act.

That's all well and good once your relationship's under way. But how to start things off on the right high-heeled foot? First, let me introduce you to the MSD glossary of frequently used relationship terms. (And, yes, there will be a quiz.)

TERMS TO LIVE BY

RFR: *Rapid Fire Response.* Without pause, without thinking, and without a glitch in your voice, you must always be ready to respond to your man. It will keep him reeling.

411: *Information.* This is crucial to gather (through whatever manipulation or coercion is required) if you're going to find out what's really going on in your relationship.

GTWTD: *Get Them While They're Down.* Throw salt in their wounds—it's the perfect way to keep the flame burning and the power on your side.

OWT: *Outwhip Them.* Make him your slave, or he'll make you his. Remember this; it's my favorite slogan.

NMW: *No Matter What.* It's the bottom line. It's what you *must* do, and I don't want to hear any complaints about it, girls. Now, let's say that you really like a guy. How to keep him on his toes NMW:

TFFSFHF: Throw Fake Fights and Stage Fake Hissy Fits. Girls, let's face it: unless your man is the leader of some religious cult or an exec from the PAX channel, men don't really like those wimpy little *Rebecca of Sunnybrook Farm* types. In the real world, if you fail to provide a little drama from time to time, your man will be bored out of his fucking mind—and, before you know it, out of the bedroom as well. Face it: how many times have we all said, *I was so nice—how could he leave me for that evil bitch?* Easy answer: you gave him no challenge, and he started to feel like he was falling into an early grave. He activated the escape hatch, leaving you digging through a box of Kleenex.

That situation doesn't have to happen as long as you ignore that nice gene and learn how to shake things up. The first step is to fake a nice fight on occasion.

For instance, take the time with my ex-man-of-the-moment that I mentioned earlier. When he failed to call during our regularly scheduled calling time, I was a little pissed. So first I ignored him for a day, which prompted him to call three times in a row. Then, when he finally got me on the line, I staged a fake fight that he walked right into.

The perfect getup for hooking your man.

"Janice, we need to talk," he said. "Why haven't you called me back?"

"Do you want to drop me?" I blurted out, interrupting him.

"No!" he said, sounding confident, like he was back in control.

"Do you want to *marry* me?" I said without missing a beat. (That's RFR in action for you, ladies!) Now he was spinning.

"No!" he said—so I hung up on him. If you're going to throw a monkey wrench into the works, you might as well toss it hard, where it will hurt the most.

By this point, the guy was cascading down a black hole. The upshot: he hopped on the next plane to L.A. to see me and make sure everything was okay. After a few hours of makeup sex, it was just fine, thank you very much (thanks to my little fake hissy fit, that is).

The bottom line is, guys want to fight as much as chicks do. It keeps their blood pumping. It's just that most of the time, it's up to the woman to light the match. We've got to shift the energy, and men are very sensitive to that dynamic in the relationship. They feel your moves. Most of the time they know when you're fucking around or just downright lying, but they like the challenge. Plus, it gives them a chance to placate you, which they love doing anyway.

So how do you do it? A little bit of RFR, for one thing. You need to have a comeback ready for every occasion, every bend in the road. When you're throwing down with your man, there's no time to stop and think, or call your girlfriend for pointers. You need to master your own shock techniques until they just flow out of your mouth *without hesitation*.

It's homework time at MSD: Here are a few instructive case studies for you to memorize (and take to heart).

SCENARIO 1

He says: "Baby, you spent an awful lot of money this weekend. Do you really need to drop four hundred bucks every time you get your hair done?"

You say: "It's *unbelievable*, I know it. But this is what I do to look good for you. I do it all for you, baby!'"

He says: "But I gave you two hundred bucks for groceries. Now we only have one moldy brick of cheddar cheese and wilted lettuce in the house. How could this be?"

You *don't* say: "I put this in my secret stash for breast implants and Botox."

Instead you say: "Baby, I didn't want to tell you, but on the way to the market I was held up at gunpoint. Now I need money for a new wallet *and* those groceries. Maybe we should just skip the market; why don't you take me out to a four-star restaurant so I can get over the shock of it all?"

SCENARIO 2

He says: "I just got my tickets for Vegas for that all-guys' weekend I was telling you about. I know you think it'll be nothing but nonstop strippers, but that's just your imagination working overtime."

You say: "Oh, I don't mind, honey. When do you leave?"

He says: "Friday afternoon at five. Try not to get too lonely without me."

You say: "Oh, don't worry about me. All my lesbian lovers should be stopping by around seven."

SCENARIO 3

He says: "I'm going out to dinner with my best friend Gillian tomorrow. Now, I don't want you to get jealous about this: remember, she's just a friend."

You say: "Hmm. *Gillian*. I remember her. Wasn't she that bikini model?"

He says: "Yeah. But she's really got a terrific personality."

You say, "How nice for you two. You know, I feel the same way about my friend Ben. He asked me out for a friendly drink tomorrow night; I guess I'm free now. Hope his girlfriend J.Lo doesn't mind." (Tip: Immediately start an affair with someone else, but do not tell him.)

SCENARIO 4

He says: "Honey, I honestly didn't know what to get you for your birthday. I hope you like this food processor."

You say: "Excuse me a moment." Go to your bedroom, close the door so he can't hear you, then pick up the phone and send yourself some long-stemmed elephant roses with a card signed *Love, You Know Who.* Display prominently upon arrival.

SCENARIO 5

He says: "Baby, I love you. But I need time to think about where this relationship is going."

You say: "Lose my number."

He says: "What if we just see other people? You know you're the only one I care for."

You say: "Sven, you're the only one! [Say it even if he's not; what's good for the goose is not good for the gander.] Baby, sunbeams come out of your eyes. Moonbeams come out of your asshole. I adore you, baby. And if this is really how you feel, too . . . then lose my number."

SCENARIO 6

He says: "Are you seeing someone else?"

You say: "Well, not yet. But it's funny you ask—I *have* been having a lot of lesbian thoughts lately." (Yes, you can turn anything into sex talk. Drop this little winner and he'll soon forget the original question.)

SCENARIO 7

He says: "We need to talk."

You say: "Do you want to dump me? Do you want to marry me?"

I don't know what good this kind of crazy-girl insecurity will do you in the long run, but in the moment it can be so damn *satisfying*. If that fails, break down in hysterics. You'll be back on top before he can say, *Come on, honey, it's all right. Let's you and I sit down with Harry Winston and talk this over.*

If these don't work, just keep trying. Don't give up—hang onto that upper hand. Remember one thing: this is war. And there's no fucking around in war.

Lots of women friends have come to me with problems like this:

"Janice, my boyfriend just spent seventy-two hours with a stripper. I've taken your advice; I'm not speaking to him. But I'm so tempted to call him. Whenever my mind wanders, I find my fingers dialing his number on an invisible cell phone keypad. What should I do?"

Dolls, it's called *diversion*. MSD's military diversion tactics will keep you in circulation while he's out in the doghouse, so you don't spend all your time working your way through ten ass-pounds of Godiva. Visit your annoying sister. Take a walk in the park—but whatever you do, *don't pick up that phone!*

Here are a few diversion tactics for when your man screws up:

Have Miniflirtations: I'm not saying you have to end up naked in bed with the FedEx guy. But it doesn't hurt to go to Starbucks and flirt with the cute guy in the Barney's suit. It keeps you in practice, and it's harmless. Plus, a little male attention when you're at your lowest never hurts.

Use Your Gay Friends: When you're seriously pissed at your boyfriend, pull a *Will & Grace*. At this point in the game, you'll find that your gay male friends have never been more valuable. Dress them up (they'll love it—trust me) and take them out with you, pretending they're potential boyfriends. Guaranteed, they'll be better-mannered, more attentive, and better color-coordinated than any hetero lover. When you hear that your boyfriend's going insane over reports that you were seen at the Ivy with a handsome guy whose Armani jacket cost more than your boyfriend makes in a month, just sit back and smile.

Be a Free Agent (at Least Verbally): During a break, when friends who know my boyfriend ask me if we've broken up, I sigh and simply say, "I guess I'm still waiting for the love of my life to show up." It's not really an answer, but it makes people wonder.

Work on Your Bod: In times of mental anguish, it helps to sweat it out. I'll grab a girlfriend who's going through her own emotional turmoil and drag her to a very long yoga class, or take her on a hike until our feet fall off. Start a kickboxing class. Sign up for moon-rocket training. (Remember, *anything's* better than returning his calls). Even better, stage a girls' night out and go dancing. All of this serves a dual purpose: while you're making your boyfriend wait, you'll also drop three or four pounds, so you'll look amazing when he comes back.

Spa It Out: While you're working so hard on your bod, you might as well engage in facials, nighttime masks, exfoliating—whatever it takes. Go to work on those grubby feet, too. In Operation Total Babe, your mission is head-to-toe perfection.

Drop Names: During the freeze-out period, be sure you make it known to his friends that you're working on a new business deal, going out every night with friends, and having mysterious business appointments with George Clooney. Drag out the juiciest names you can—even if they seem ridiculous. This will require lying and making stuff up, but who cares? All's fair in love and war. Whether you say the prince of Spain is coming over for a twelve-course dinner, or the Dalai Lama is giving up his calling to come to America to do you, just sprinkle in the names of a few good men wherever they fit in. It'll drive him *nuts*.

May I Remind You: *Don't* return his calls or e-mails, even when it seems like the floodgates have opened. Stay away from places where you'll bump into him. Tell your mutual friends you're going to Aspen for a ski vacation. He needs to remember he's entered the territory known as **DS,** or Deep Shit.

Eventually, of course, there's always the chance you'll take him back. (What else is all that game-playing for, but to give you the chance to *decide* whether he's good enough to take back—and on what terms?) But what do you do when he falls back into his stupid old ways?

Let's say he says something really hurtful. How to handle, Janice?

First of all, remind yourself of one thing: men are pigs. They *say* stupid things. It's a hobby of theirs. One friend of mine had a boyfriend who told her that she wasn't "the grand passion" of his life—that they shouldn't necessarily break up, just "reevaluate their relationship."

"Janice, what should I *dooooo?*" she wailed.

"School of discipline, babe," I responded. "Make him pay for that. You set the punishment."

If a guy says something to me that I don't like, I save it under "Moronic Men Comments," a special file I keep in the back of my head. While filing, I smile my sexiest grin and lick my lips, like a she-wolf catching first sight of her dinner. Then I refer to one of the cardinal rules of MSD: *Make yourself totally unavailable, but don't be a bitch about it.* If he happens to get you on the phone, just say, "Oh my God, I'm so busy." Again, the real trick is not to return his calls—sometimes for a week, and sometimes for a month.

This reminds me of the time when I practically tortured a major entertainment executive (we'll call him Jack)—who, incidentally, totally deserved it. Of course, he kept calling, and calling, and calling. Finally, about a month later, I consented to let him take me out to a fabulous dinner, where Jack looked completely depressed over his tomato basil salad and the best Merlot on the list.

"Janice, I just have to ask one thing of you," he begged. "Would you please return my calls?" It was almost too sad. I just looked at him with my big baby browns and replied, "Oh, you called?"

"About a hundred times," he stammered. I just smiled. He must have gotten the message, and then some: next time we had dinner he was even more desperate.

"Janice, why don't we just get married and combine our chaos?" he implored.

"What an emotional way to profess your love," I replied, noncommittal yet inwardly satisfied. The school of discipline had obviously worked, maybe a little too well . . .

Look, I'll crazy-glue your fingers together, ladies, if you play into the games these jokers play. When you're really pissed at them, I forbid you to make a single move in their direction. Let them come to you—because they will, each and every time. I promise.

The real question is: Will you still want them?

In certain situations, you've really got to weigh your options carefully. Is it worth keeping him? Or is it time to toss him to the curb? Consider:

Catching Your Guy Fucking Someone Else: It's the worst—the ultimate flying side kick to your solar plexus. Is it forgivable? Oh, yeah. Men are fucked up; they do as many stupid things as they say. Still, give yourself some time to decide whether you really want this dog back in your house. Could you stand to catch him cheating again? Because it'll probably (make that *definitely*) happen. Guys like this are usually a shit storm just waiting to brew up, and you have to figure out how much you hate getting caught in the crap.

Decide That Every Romance Doesn't Have to Be True Love: Sometimes men are just for sport—especially when we're talking about your average whiskey-drinking, Wall Street-vibing, girl-playing, SUV-driving, football-obsessed, all-American male. I go through periods where I'm just totally bored with the whole chase for the true love of my life. It's *okay* to admit that sometimes you just want one thing—a little good old-fashioned fucking. (Don't give me that shocked expression. We all think it; I just have the guts to say it.)

Invent Imaginary Lovers: Let's say that true love is what you want. But your lover has screwed up, and yet you still want him back. How do you prolong the torture?

What you need is an imaginary lover. Think of him as a sexier version of your imaginary friend from childhood.

First, send yourself two dozen roses, boxes of Godiva, maybe a little expensive lingerie. Gaze softly at your shithead boyfriend and say, "Oh, babe, thank you so much. It's the most luxurious, slinkiest, sexiest nightie any man has ever given me."

Look just slightly guilty when he stammers, "But I didn't send that to you."

Then gasp like you've been caught doing something semiawful. Tell him it must have been a screwup at FedEx. Then go into the other room—leaving the door ajar—and pretend to call your girlfriend, in a bellowing stage whisper. "Oh my God, Tiffany! You remember that Italian race car driver we met last month? What was his name again? Why won't he leave me alone? I *told* him I wasn't going with him to Italy for the summer."

Listen for the sound of your boyfriend's eyes popping out of his sorry skull.

How to Handle Other Bitches Who Are After Your Guy: Once again, everything you need to know about dating can be learned at the local pet store. As a woman, you've got to nudge the other puppies out of the way if you want to get a shot at the nipple. Girls, do what you must to push the other bitches aside. A little rumor of herpes, for example, can do wonders.

Of course, all these games don't mean anything if the relationship really doesn't deserve to be saved. How do you handle that kind of heartbreak?

If He Still Doesn't Pass: Look for someone else. Whatever you do, though, don't believe this crap that you can be friends with your ex. You'll end up feeling like you're living in the Twilight Zone—or a bad episode of *Sex and the City*—and, frankly, who needs to hang out with that alien species known as "the boyfriend gone bad"? Move on, honey.

Just Don't Go Too Far: Once I announced to an annoying boyfriend who was leaving that I didn't really care if he was out the door because I was sleeping with . . . *Bill Clinton*. (Can you imagine the megalomaniac brain that could whip that out on the spot as an RFR? Watch and learn, ladies.)

The guy actually believed me. When we made up the following month, though, I admitted I'd never been with Bill. He just looked at me with great concern. "Honey, you don't have to explain it to me," he said. "I'm not mad about you and Bill, but I would prefer if we just didn't talk about it. You're my girlfriend; he's my President. I can't handle the thought of the two of you together." He was actually jealous!

The following Sunday morning, when Clinton showed up on TV, my squeeze leaned over to me in bed and said, "Baby, he didn't talk about trade treaties with you, did he?" I sunk down in the covers, pretending to smother myself. I think he took that as a *no*.

More on Breaking Up

Breakups happen to all of us. We don't live in a perfect universe where people act exactly the way we want them to. And men can barely act like human beings, so naturally every so often they're going to throw us over the edge—and *kaboom!* There goes the entire relationship.

It's not easy to get through the fallout, and you can't fake it and pretend that everything is fine when you feel like screaming at the moon. The key is to try to look at the situation rationally.

START BY STOPPING

Stopping what? Trying to figure out why he did what he did, and what you did to deserve it. You could spend the rest of your life trying to solve this mystery—and while you're at it the rest of your life is ticking by. You might as well put your time into figuring out who killed JFK, or how to get everyone in the Middle East to kiss and make up. There's no point in scraping around at the bottom of a big, bottomless pit.

So repeat after me: "Janice, I'll stop."

DON'T PROJECT

At this point, if you've got any kind of imagination, you'll be tempted to start making up nasty, paranoid little fantasies about what he's doing now that he's on his own. *Delete that shit.* I know you're convinced that he's

Three sets of twelve, three times a week ought to do the trick.

banging that bitch down the hallway who was always coming over in her towel to borrow something. And maybe they *are* swinging from the ceiling fan, but who really gives a damn? Stop trying to figure out what he's doing night and day. Do this by remembering and saying the following statement out loud: "I am so much more important than his daily activities. I must let go and not think about this anymore because it's going to get me a one-way ticket to the loony bin, where I'll be stuck wearing some unflattering, white jacket."

So repeat after me: "Janice, I'll stop."

IT'S ALL ABOUT YOU

Whatever you do, do *not* stop working out and taking care of yourself. Oh, don't get me wrong: I understand the urge to give up. We've all been there. Once you don't have a boyfriend anymore, it's easy to say, "Fuck Pilates—who's going to be running their hands over my stomach or kissing my toned thighs anyway?" But this is stupid thinking, and here's why: your brain and emotions will be on the mend much faster if you keep up the physical activity. Just because men are pigs doesn't mean you have to turn into a little piglet by camping out at the Dairy Queen.

Ladies, if you're thinking about taking a little trip down that long carbo highway, take my advice and get out of the car. If you've already made it to the drive-through, pull away from that window before you get hurt. Start respecting yourself—and working on that muscle tone before it deserts you (*desserts* you?) like another stinking man.

So repeat after me: "Janice, I'll start."

LOOK AROUND, BUT CAREFULLY

The best way to get over a breakup, of course, is to find someone new—and you can't do that if you're still down for the count, right? So, Robin

Redbreasts, the only thing to do is go back out into the field, knowing that you're such a hot chick that guys should be chasing *you*. Start being seen around town. Start letting your friends know you're looking. Start living your life again.

So repeat after me: "Janice, I'll start."

And when you find better, you'll know.

We all know everything's better when you're in love. Blame the chemicals or the hormones, but that feeling is what drives us as human beings. Centuries ago, before we started fighting over oil, men went to war for love. Poets have died for love, and so have supermodels.

But not this supermodel. And not you, either. Got it? Now get over it.

12.

Perfect Men Who Have Captured My Fancy (or Not)

"Hi, Big Dick," he said, as if it were an acceptable form of greeting.

No, you won't find Jack Nicholson's nickname for me sanctioned by Miss Manners as a quick way to shout out a hello. But what do you want? Jack's a born rule-breaker—and when it comes to the Big Dick part . . . well, he's very well endowed in the sense of humor department.

As for me, I'd just snort at him. Here was Bad Boy Jack, a guy who was arguably the most talented actor on the planet. And he knew he could turn that charm on and off whenever he wanted. Still, when we dated he wasn't as wrapped up in himself as you might think. He didn't have the smarmy ego that just blows it for so many other guys.

Just in case you're still laboring under any illusions about the rich and famous, let me indulge in a little reminiscing—and show you how the Big Dog separates the wheat from the chaff.

An Offer I Could Refuse

When I went on a date with Robert Duvall, he took me to the historic Roosevelt Hotel on Hollywood Boulevard for dinner and dancing. For some reason, Bob (as he likes to be called) reminded me of my father, which really scared the shit out of me. Why? Maybe because of his serious tone of voice. Maybe the way he kept barking at me: "I'm going to do this incredible movie! I'm going to do this *movie!*"

Calm down, Mr. Acting Legend, I thought. *Don't have a heart attack.* I could see it all now, playing out in the tabloids: "*Godfather* Star Keels Over at Feet of World's First Supermodel."

Our first drinks had just arrived when he started in with his pitch. "Baby, I'm going to do this tango movie, and I want you to star in it!" Duvall said over our first drink, and my jaw almost dropped. I thought this was just dinner, not a job offer. Yet here was Robert Duvall, his pulse racing over some new film called *Assassination Tango.*

"Bob, I'm not an actress. I'm a supermodel," I reminded him. An hour later, I was still repeating those words—while eating my dinner as slowly as possible. (I had a feeling he was hoping to get a little touchy-feely during my tango "lesson.")

"Sure, you're not an actress *now*," he boomed. "By the time our movie comes out, though, you *will* be an actress. And you *will* be in this movie!"

Yeah, right, I thought. "Could you hold that thought while I use the ladies' room?"

"No time for a break," Duvall said, grabbing my hand and leading me to the dance floor, where he was going to tango me until my name was right up there with his on the marquee. The band started playing, and Bob started swaying. It only took seconds for my own feet to betray me. When Bob tried to sweep me up into a twirl, I almost landed on my ass.

Let me put it bluntly: I can't fucking tango. I could barely even get down the end of a runway. My most famous runway move was falling off and landing in poor Sophia Loren's lap. Now I was facing a very annoyed movie star who was about to grab a rose and put it between his teeth.

"Honey, everything I do, I make sure I excel at it. You will, too. You'll *be* in my movie, and you'll be a *wonderful* tango dancer! You'll even start to *go out* with me!"

Holy shit—would this guy ever stop yelling? I was convinced he was going to have a stroke before we even got to dessert.

"I'll be right back, Bobby," I purred, and I left him on the dance floor.

It just so happened that my friend Garth Murphy was also having

Blond power. BAM!

dinner at the Roosevelt, and he was watching the entire situation go down (downhill, that is) from the corner of his very amused eye. When I abandoned Duvall and made a run for the lobby, Garth followed me, cracking up all the while. "Janice, I know you're going to ditch this guy," he said. "So can you do me a favor first? Can you please go back in there and ask him to say the line 'Charlie don't surf' from *Apocalypse Now?*"

So I dragged Garth back into the dining room. Duvall was still on the dance floor practicing his moves by himself, oblivious to the fact that he was on the verge of being ditched.

"Bob, this is my friend. Could you say this line from *Apocalypse Now?*"

"Charlie don't surf," he repeated, a little confused.

"Thanks. But I still can't be in your tango movie," I said, turned on my heel, and left.

I think Bobby D wanted to get laid that night, but I didn't take him up on it—screen legend or not. When I glanced back, he was still on the dance floor, all alone. No one was going to boss me around that way on a date. Tango *this*, pal.

Postscript: Bob eventually cast a woman he met at a bakeshop in Argentina in the film. Now she's living with him. I hope the poor girl's got a pair of industrial-strength earplugs.

Dust in the Wind

If you want a great diva story, let's talk about my one date with Charlie Sheen. I ran into the handsome Brat Packer back in the 1990s when I was walking out of Giuseppe Franko's hair salon in Hollywood. Sheen, who was hot off the movies *Major League* and *Platoon*, stopped dead in his tracks, gave me the slow once-over, and said in his whispery, angst-ridden voice, "You. Me. Us. Let's have dinner."

Another Celeb Big Shot who couldn't handle a proper introduction. But I just smiled—he was handsome, rich, and famous; that's the law in Hollywood—and decided to give the guy a break and break a little bread with him. First step: get his number. I fished around my purse in vain. "Sorry, I don't have anything to write on."

"Well, neither do I," he said, flashing that killer smile that worked on Jennifer Grey when he played the bad boy in the police station in *Ferris Bueller's Day Off*.

A man of action (in more ways than one), Charlie reached deep into his 501s and pulled out a fresh twenty-dollar bill. He proceeded to rip it in half with great gusto.

"I'm going to write my number on this half of the twenty. When I see you later, I'll give you the other half and you can help pay for dinner," he announced.

Now, there was a guy with a sense of humor. Apparently Mr. Sheen Senior had raised his boy right.

As the sun dipped below the mountains that night, I pulled up to the out-of-the-way little sushi restaurant we'd chosen just outside of Los Angeles. There was no sign of Charlie, so I walked inside, asked for a quiet table, and ordered us a bottle of sake. An hour passed, and so did that bottle. I ordered another.

What kept me from leaving the restaurant and hating Charlie Sheen for the rest of my life remains a mystery. At the time I was appearing nearly every month on the cover of a major magazine near you; he was a B-movie actor at best. How dare he stand me up! I sat there trying to figure that one out—until I suddenly noticed a stretch limo that must have been three city blocks long pull up outside this tiny sushi joint. Charlie ambled into the restaurant, two hours late and clearly blitzed out of his mind.

"Pretty baby," he said, leaning closer to me and smelling like a six-pack of cheap beer died in his mouth. "I got coke out in the limo. Fuck this place."

By this time I was so mad that I was beyond screaming. I wanted a better kind of revenge, so I slid my miniskirted ass into that leather limo seat as he salivated away.

I nodded when he pulled out a huge silver tray filled with a mountain of coke that he had saved "for our party."

"Ch-ch-ch-Charlie, that was ssoo-ss—" I gasped . . . then screwed up my face and landed a fake sneeze smack-dab in the middle of that tray of coke, just like Woody Allen. Charlie's drug of choice blew all over that rental car. Let's just say it was the only thing blown that night.

Moral of the story, boys: Don't keep the Big Dog waiting.

Donald Trumped

Let's go back to New York. January 1980. It was snowing hard; the temperature was way below freezing. It was one of those nights when there were no taxis around, so I told myself that hoofing it around the city was just one more of life's many benefits. Instant cardio: no need to go to the gym. Hell, I'd been sweating it out dancing at Studio 54 earlier that evening; maybe I'd never exercise again!

By 2:00 A.M., I'd trudged my way back to this loft where I was staying with a photographer friend. Glad to be back in the warmth of his living room, I plopped down on the couch—and that's when the doorbell rang. It was Selma, one of my model friends.

"Janice, aren't you bored out of your fucking mind?"

That sounded like a dare to me. So, like two mental cases, we wandered back out into the freezing night.

A few streets away, we came across this lovely Italian restaurant that was still open. The minute we stepped inside, two handsome, fortyish businessmen fell all over each other buying us a bottle of Cristal. By this point I was glad to take a load off, warm up, and have a drink. An hour later, we shucked off the guys, and the cold wintry blast hit us hard on the way out the door. At the time I had 0 percent body fat; I was so cold I honestly didn't think I would make it home.

Opportunity has a strange way of presenting itself. Through my tearing eyes, I noticed a beautiful black stretch limo outside, parked and running. Tapping on the window, I got ready to beg the driver for a ride home. But there was no driver in sight.

"Come on, Selma," I said to my model friend. "We're taking this limo."

"They're giving us a ride home?" she said hopefully.

"No, we're giving us a ride home," I replied.

I was Thelma and Selma was Louise when I jumped into the driver's seat. My girlfriend took her cue and sat in the back, as if this were her very own car and hopping into it was the most natural thing in the entire world.

"Ohhhh, there's a phone," Selma cried from the back.

"Do not use the phone!" I barked. Even in my drunken state I knew that'd be the easiest way to get our asses caught.

Miraculously, I managed to drive that hulk a few blocks—and then park it, which was even tougher. I threw the keys in the front seat and we went back into my photographer friend's loft, ready to hit the sack. He was waiting up for us, though, so I told him the story. He ran outside to take a peek at the car and glance around for any sign of the police.

He was breathless when he returned. "Do you know whose car you stole, Janice?"

I shrugged. It's not like I had time to read the vehicle registration. Grand theft auto's a busy lifestyle, chump.

"That car belongs to Donald Trump!" he yelled.

"Well, that's a relief," I said, mustering a little bravado. "The Donald can certainly afford another car." I swallowed hard, then went to bed. I figured that was as safe a place as any to be when the cops came bursting in to arrest me.

Nothing happened that night, strangely enough, and in the morning the car was gone. End of story? Not for Janice.

Not long after that, having decided it wasn't so great being an alcoholic anymore, I went into recovery. One of the many steps I had to take, of course, was to confess my previous wrongdoings. God, there was a prospect: I could get a full-time job apologizing.

A few weeks later, I was at a Vera Wang fashion show in Manhattan. Holding my glass of water, I glanced around . . . and in the corner, sipping a vodka tonic, was none other than The Donald.

Time to make amends.

"Hello," Trump said when I approached, his eyes lively and open for business.

"Look, I'm going to cut to the chase," I rambled. "I'm really sorry, but I'm the girl who took your limo a few weeks ago." Trump had that hard look on his face; I wasn't sure if he was going to kiss me or kill me. So I just kept blabbering while The Donald looked at me, quite perplexed.

"I figured I'd wait for the statute of limitations to run out before I confessed all!" I blurted, wondering if he could still have me busted.

Trump slapped the sides of his Hugo Boss suit and laughed so hard I thought he might need medical attention. He was so cool about the whole situation that I liked him instantly. "That's the best story I've ever heard," he told me.

"I'm *really* sorry. But I was drunk that night, and now I'm in recovery. This is part of my process—confessing my sins. I'm so sorry I stole your car."

"Now you've stolen my heart," he said, winking.

Stitching Up Bruno

After living in New York for a while, I got pretty sick of the constant parade of slick industry types and tedious business executives. One night, though, fate smiled on me—in the shape of this completely unpretentious, beefy-looking bartender from New Jersey named Bruce. He was your average guy's guy—with a twist. Instead of planning to pour beers until he could own the bar, Bruno (as his Joisey friends called him) wanted to become a famous actor. *Yeah, right,* I thought. *What a dreamer! There's already one famous Bruce from Jersey. What are the chances of two?*

One thing led to another; our conversation led to the bedroom. He was a fabulous snuggler, so big and brawny. I just tucked myself right into his chest, clamped safely in place by those biceps like a Ferrari secured by The Club. What could I do but purr in contentment and listen?

VOGUE
VOGUE BEAUTÉ

F 30

SPÉCIAL

1000 CONSEILS POUR L'ÉTÉ

Thrilled to have nailed another cover.

This was shot by the master of masters—you know who he is. This was my first headshot for *Vogue*.

Gerber cheeks—hot as Hell.

The master, Versace, and I collaborated on this campaign, which has gone
down in the fashion archives of photo history. One of my all-time faves.

At a very young stage in my modeling career. I felt a little _under_whelmed knowing I couldn't fill out that brassiere. Another attack of prediction anxiety. Where were my falsies when I needed them? PHOTOGRAPH BY MITCHEL GRAY

Between Valentino and Scavullo, how can a girl go wrong?

You've got to admit, it's getting better. It's getting better all the time.

What's up, doc? Where's the local disco?

In Scavullo's studio it's all about the photo. Carol Alt doesn't hurt.

It's raining men. Hallelujah!

NOT JUST MOIST.
NOT JUST MORE MOIST.
BUT 83% MOISTURIZERS.
FOR 100% TERRIFIC LIPS.

TAKE YOUR LIPS
TO THE

Maxi-Moist
Lipstick

Where's the rest of the outfit? Must have forgotten to pick it up at the dry cleaners. . . .

Foxy Lady!

This was Sante D'Orazio's first *Bazaar* shoot. I knew from the first
frame that the kid stays in the picture. Attitude, attitude, attitude.
You go, diva!

Phillip Dixon coaxed my facial expression into pensive, toxic radioactive. *Elle* magazine au Paris!

What you don't know is that that bathing suit was pinned up the wazoo for days! I don't know how I pulled it off. Thank God for growing up in Hollywood, Florida. The perfect body for haute couture. Eat your heart out, Giselle and Naomi!

To have the most easy, breezy look, we faced temperatures in the teens. Freezing our skinny little butts off—another pitfall of modeling.

In 2003, before Artefill. California, age forty-eight. And away we go to erase the wrinkles . . .

Before surgery.

The perfect no-makeup accessory? Smile! (It's free.)

A look behind the scenes—what it takes to be perfect.

A personal fave. Annie get your gun. Creating an ambiance by
suggesting a little hanky-panky. Whew! PHOTOGRAPH BY ISABEL SNYDER

I love my job. I love my family. I love my life. PHOTOGRAPH BY MARK GIARD

Feeling fine at forty-nine. It's all about love and the ability to hang on to what you've got.

PHOTOGRAPH BY

MARK GIARD

Isabel Snyder really captured the essence of pain.

PHOTOGRAPH BY ISABEL SNYDER

What's for dinner, darling? Pass the mouthwash!

PHOTOGRAPH BY ISABEL SNYDER

The millennium English *Vogue* issue on the hottest models in history, shot by Nick Knight. He captured my essence. PHOTOGRAPH BY NICK KNIGHT

My boyfriend, Rip, witnessed me doing yoga in this same Dolce and Gabbana vintage piece before an episode of *Rock Me Baby*. What was I supposed to do with the perfect black evening dress?

The Dickinson clan. Here we are on a holiday in Hawaii (right). My kids, Savvy and Nathan, have everything. PHOTOGRAPH AT LEFT BY MARK GIARD

"Someday I'm going to have my name in huge letters on a movie poster, Janice," Bruce Willis would tell me.

"Sounds like a great dream," I'd tell him. Secretly, though, I wondered about his chances. As cute as he was to me, I wasn't sure America wanted their movie men to look like bruisers who poured beers for a living.

We hung out for that entire summer; then the still-unfamous Bruce Willis moved in with me. The only problem was, I'd painted my bedroom a perfect Diana Vreeland bitch red. I loved it—but the vibe in there never allowed me to sleep. I thought I was in Hell: all night I laid awake thinking *red rum . . . red rum . . .*

At first Bruce thought it was cool, too. But I think it threw his sleep patterns off, too—and soon I began seeing little hints of anger spilling out from his subconscious during the day.

One day in Central Park, I found out that Bruno was tougher than I'd even thought possible. It started out simply enough: he was playing softball in some league, and I tagged along to use the bleachers to do sit-ups and push-ups and work my triceps. Afterward, Bruce and I were walking down Columbus Avenue when some Joe Palooka type passed us and made a big show out of giving me the slow once-over. When he winked at me, I could tell Bruce was about to explode.

"What are you doing?" he screamed. "She's *my* fucking girlfriend!"

The guy took a quick step to the left and got directly in Bruce's face. "You wanna do something about it?" Joe Palooka asked Mr. *Die Hard*–to-be. Then, before I could blink, Joe instigated a flying side kick and implanted his foot in the right side of my honey's bloody lip. Yes, Bruce Willis was knocked on his ass by a nobody.

A little blood didn't stop Mr. Willis from jumping up and screaming, "I'll kill you, you motherfucker!" He was out of his fucking mind. Suddenly the future Mr. *Moonlighting* was chasing Joe down the street, with three busboys from a nearby Chinese restaurant dogging his heels for good measure. It's a good thing Palooka was fast because Bruce had trouble in his eyes. Not only was he still bleeding, he was *embarrassed*. His job was to protect his supermodel, and he had failed.

When Bruce finally came back, I started wiping away his blood with my bare hand. I knew we needed to get some serious medical help, so I dragged Bruno to Lenox Hill Hospital, where a Puerto Rican doctor friend of mine was head of the emergency room. I knew he'd be able to take care of Bruce in a way that I would want my own face cared for after a kung fu attack.

I took charge as soon as we arrived. "Put away that regular needle," I told the nurses. "This man needs a plastic surgery needle on his lip. He's going to be a famous movie star one day." I still wasn't sure Bruce would ever make it as an actor, but something deep inside triggered my perfection hormones. It wasn't so much that I couldn't be with a guy who had a lip scar. I just kept imagining that scar on a forty-foot movie screen and wincing.

Later that night, while he was recovering from multiple stitches and still groggy from all the pain meds, I stepped in as Nancy Nurse. This was in the most nonsexual way possible. Propped up on about a million bitch-red pillows, Bruce smiled that wiseguy little grin and said, "I hope it leaves a little mark. That will forever be known as 'the Janice Dickinson scar.'"

"From the day you saved my life from a crazy killer," I responded, caressing his beefy arm and making him feel like the man he thought he was being on those streets. Funny, that was the man he would be in movies someday where he *really* saved the girl—without the help of a team of rabid busboys.

Years later I named my beloved dog after Bruce. Bruno Dickinson was a fine Labrador retriever with a bit of a messed-up lip, but a brave spirit. He even went after a guy who was pestering me on the street, just like you-know-who.

Recently I ran into his two-legged namesake at Ago, a trendy spot in Beverly Hills. "Remember the red room?" he asked, leaning down to give me a peck on the cheek.

"Do you remember the stitches?" I responded, noticing his pristine kisser. "You owe me," I tossed out. "You could have been Scarface Willis."

Mr. Movie Star just smiled and walked away, rejoining his posse of fawners.

My girlfriend came up to me after Willis was gone. "He should get back together with Demi," she whispered. "Don't you think?"

"Nah, I don't think so," I replied. "Once the party's over, it's over."

Blind Date with Destiny

One night during the lackluster 1980s, Kenny Austin, the youngest son of Mo Austin of Warner Brothers Records, told me to meet him at the Monkey Bar at nine; he had someone who wanted to meet me. It was just a few months after I'd divorced my husband, producer Simon Fields, and we were going through a nasty child custody battle over our son, Nathan.

A little dejected from all the personal mess in my life, I thought about staying in. But then I figured, *What the hell? If I'm going to be depressed, I might as well do it on the town.* So that night I showed up at the Four Seasons restaurant in Beverly Hills with my chin cast downward—until I noticed the man Kenny'd set up to be my dinner companion for the night. None other than Mr. George Harrison.

The beautiful brunette actress Joan Severance sat on his other side, but George rarely even glanced her way, much to her great dismay. He seemed captivated with me, which was odd because suddenly I snapped out of my funk and began grilling him about all the old Beatle songs. "What was your inspiration for 'Michelle'?" I drilled him. (Should have asked Paul, I know.) "What did it feel like when you did *The Ed Sullivan Show* for the first time?" I felt like Barbara Walters.

I have to give it to George. Not only was he sweet and polite; not only did he answer every stupid question I asked; not only did he spill the details; no, he *made me laugh.* And he made me feel like he was really sharing something special with me. This man had been my idol since I was stuffing my training bra. I was going out of my mind.

This is the second Beatle I've met, and I've slept with a Rolling Stone. Does life get any sweeter?

After dinner we moved into the Monkey Bar. A member of our party decided it was too overwhelming to be out in public with George, and suggested that we go back to his room at the Bel-Air.

"Why not?" George said.

"If we go, you have to play some music for me," I begged. "Please, George?"

"For you, anything," he said with a twinkle in his eye, and as soon as we got there, George and I moved into his room to carry on our little party of two.

For hours on end I just sat on the sunken leather couch in his hotel room while George Harrison serenaded me. The only instrument he had on hand was a ukulele, but I made him play every Beatles song ever written. He didn't even seem to mind; he just played on and on.

Around two in the morning, I got a crazy idea. "Hey, George, do you have any idea where Paul is? Can we *call* him?"

"I don't see why not," he said, as if he were giving me an update on the weather. "He's just in the next room."

Get out! George just shrugged, lifted the receiver, and dialed a few digits. Once Paul answered, George announced, "Paul, I've got a bird here who'd really like to say hi to you."

He handed me the phone, and for once my own hand began to shake a bit. Here was a moment I'd been waiting for my entire life. I was on the phone with Paul McCartney. Was this for real? At last my life was truly blessed.

"Paul, I love you so much and I'm a big fan. Do you think you could come over?" I asked, trembling and babbling.

Paul just laughed and said, "I'd love to come over, luv, but me missus wouldn't like it."

Hey, you can tell Linda I'm no homewrecker, I wanted to say. *I just wanted to meet you.* But Paul rang off.

As the sun came up and my Ten Thousand Beatle Questions finally slowed down, George yawned affectionately. "I'm going to dedicate my lifetime achievement award someday to you," he told me. "You've got to be the biggest Beatle fan I've ever met. I thought you'd never run out of questions."

"Oh, George," I purred, then thought a moment longer. "Okay, one more thing: I don't hate Yoko. Why does everyone else rip on her so much?"

George just gave me a sweet kiss on the cheek and said, "Good night, Janice." It remains one of the loveliest nights I've ever spent in a man's hotel room.

The One Who Got Away

Just in case you're thinking I've always had my pick of the litter, don't fret: there have been a few here and there who got away. A year ago, I was having dinner in Los Angeles at Ago (again). My supermodel girlfriend Nia was in town from Sweden, and I wanted to show her a good time.

While we were there, George Clooney walked his Sexiest-Ass-Alive by our table. The girl he was with was clearly his date for the evening: I could tell by the little kamikaze daggers she was shooting our way the second the two of them walked in. Ever the gentleman, George simply winked at us as he passed our table.

Until I practically screamed at him, that is. "George! *Hang on!* Where's the fire?"

Clooney just smiled, turned in midstep, and swaggered over in his Hugo Boss suit. "Ladies, how are you this evening?" he said, mentally timing the encounter so as not to upset his date. I could just see his wheels turning: *If I can deal with these girls in less than three minutes, then technically Ms. Burning Jealousy can't possibly consider it rude.*

How sad I was when he walked away because we made the type of eye contact that held on just a little too long to forget. Ladies, you know what I'm talking about: it's the difference between "have a nice day" and "I'd like to see you naked at my place by midnight."

I'm not disappointed. It ain't over till the supermodel sings.

Slick Mick, Not So Quick

Of course, I have to end this section on less-than-perfect dates with . . . Mr. Mick Jagger. When I first decided to hook up with Slick Mick, I went through a bit of a crisis. After we first met backstage at one of his L.A. shows, I knew he wanted to spend the night together. While I went through the should-I-or-shouldn't-I mental mambo, the decision was made for me by a lower power. I had just gotten my "girly girl," as I call it—my little monthly enemy. Right then, though, the enemy seemed an awful lot like a friend: I couldn't sleep with Mick Jagger while practically hemorrhaging down below, and that gave me a little time to think.

As always, I preferred to shoot from the hip. So I told Mick that sex was out for the moment—I was in the red.

"That's all right, luv," he said. "Come to the show tomorrow night and I'll dedicate a song to your period."

"*Which one?*" I demanded. Now, *this* was exciting—a little more than the thought of getting naked with him, if you want to know the truth. My period was finally getting the recognition it deserved.

"I want to surprise you, luv," Slick Mick responded.

The following night at the concert I ran into Jack Nicholson, who decided to stand so close to me I thought I'd have to have him surgically removed. He gave me the ol' eyebrow arch, but I just ignored him. I was too excited about my song to care about some movie star, especially when Mick swiveled his hips up to the mike and told the crowd of thirty thousand in Los Angeles, "I'd like to dedicate a song to a special friend. You know who you are! This is actually for *her* special friend."

With those words, he launched into the opening strains of "Let It Bleed." I just stood there contemplating my next tampon change, basking in rock heaven.

13.

Me and JFK Jr.

It was 1992. I was back in New York for a modeling gig, which seemed like a routine turn of events. One day I wandered into Frederic Fekkai to get my hair done when the famed hairdresser turned to me and said "*Daaaahling!*" (For him, that one word could be an entire sentence.) "What are you doing tonight? I have a date for you."

"He better be good," I said as one of his girls mixed up my highlights.

With a twinkle in his eyes and a sly smile, Frederic whipped me around in the stylist's chair and whispered into my ear, "Trust me. I *know* you'll like this one."

"All you French guys think just anyone will do," I griped. I ripped those pointy professional scissors out of his hands and pretended to threaten him with them. "I need a top-drawer man, Frederic," I said with all the menace I could muster.

"I assure you, Janice," Frederic said. "This is one for the books." And indeed it was.

Frederic refused to tell me exactly who I was hitting the town with that night, which made me assume he was serving me up a loser of epic proportions. No big deal, I figured: if this guy drools in his soup or has a rug made out of dog hair, I'll strong-arm Freddy into free hair care for the rest of my life.

At eight that evening I showed up at Un Deux Trois, a hot spot owned by another friend of mine (another Frederick—go figure). And there, on a bar stool, sat the man of my evening—and the man of any girl's dreams. Lo and behold, my blind date was one of the most gorgeous men I've ever seen in my entire supermodel life. (And where I work, ladies, hot guys are a dime a dozen.)

You know the name: John F. Kennedy Jr.

The moment I saw him I was spellbound—which, if you've gotten this far, you know isn't exactly my normal reaction to most men. But there he was, JFK Jr. in the flesh, in a stunning houndstooth jacket and a festive mood. Every beautiful hair on his head was in place, and that smile was like a big sexy dessert before we'd even ordered an appetizer.

Of course, I wouldn't be Janice if I hadn't started the evening out with a bit of an inappropriate comment. The moment I stared into those big famous eyes, everything around us disappeared; I could think of one person and one person alone.

Unfortunately, it wasn't my dinner date.

"So, what's it like to be Jackie O's son?" I blurted out. I couldn't help myself. I was completely taken by this man's . . . mother.

Suddenly Junior's eyes began to fall; his smile disappeared, and he looked like a puppy that had just peed on the rug.

"Tell me," I said, and he leaned closer, as if in the hope that I was finally focusing on him. "When you were a little boy," I began, and he gave me the most darling hopeful look, as if I were about to ask something

Opposite: This was for an Italian fashion magazine. Don't I look like Jackie Onassis?

profound about his deepest thoughts and dreams. "Did you ever play in Jackie O's closet?"

Junior just sat back in his chair, completely dejected.

Look, I know what you're thinking. But you've got to understand: when I was a girl, Jackie O meant everything to me. She was the personification of elegance, of taste, of everything I wanted to be. I couldn't help myself.

But my curiosity obviously confused her gorgeous son. "Hon, how did Oleg Cassini treat you?" I asked, thinking of that pink Chanel suit his mother was wearing the day his father was assassinated. Even in the most horrifying situation, his mother had been the most glamorous woman in the world. "Did she do her own hair, or was there a stylist always on call?" I asked.

Was he put off? That might be an understatement. I guess I could understand when Junior kept excusing himself during dinner to go off and use the phone.

I did have one thing going for me, though: I was looking pretty good that night in a black Valentino cocktail dress. I was also sporting my first set of boob inserts, and sitting there with John-John, I kept worrying about how they were holding up this French silk number. And I had plenty to worry about: the straps of the dress kept slipping south, no matter how I shifted to compensate.

Despite the family stuff, I still honestly thought I had a chance to sign the deal that night. If I could just get off my favorite topic, I thought, I might pull this off.

Excusing myself to go to the ladies' room, I began to form a plan. If I could only get a chance to kiss him, I might make him forget everything that came before. Luckily, who did I meet when I came out of the john but John? For some of the other bitches in that club, it was the luckiest pee of their lives; they got a brush with greatness before having a flush of solitude.

At that moment, I admired JFK Jr. in a way that few have in the past. Standing outside a ladies' room wasn't such a safe spot for a hunted hunk, but he risked it to come find me. And there he was, standing alone in his houndstooth jacket, looking delicious.

Suddenly, the Sexiest Kennedy Alive slammed me against the wall, and his beautiful lush lips were on mine. We made out for about five minutes while women who passed by struggled to contain their jealousy. "You are so damn hot," I told him when I finally came up for air—which wasn't an easy thing to do, believe me.

"Well, the so-called Sexiest Man Alive wanted to plant one on the sexiest lips alive," he responded, then French-kissed me hard. My mind was swimming with thoughts—but not all of them were what you might think. As our tongues met and he held me in his tender embrace, I wondered, *Whatever happened to Jackie O's First Lady wardrobe? If I slept with him, would he let me come over to his mother's house and touch them?* God forgive me, but that's what I was thinking while I was smooching the Prince of Camelot. So sue me.

I think he knew my attention was wandering elsewhere, and he finally broke the kiss. "You know what, Janice?" he said. "I have to go." And he was gone.

Forever.

So many questions went through my mind at that point, and they've only multiplied in the years since. What about the late beautiful Carolyn Bessette, for instance? Did she ever get to try on a few of Jackie's hats? Oh, and what was it like to sleep with JFK Jr.?

Oh, never mind that. Bring on the pillbox hats.

14

Not-So-Perfect Sex: Lust and Betrayal

Here was a *seemingly* perfect situation: a talented screenwriter who gets a million-five-plus per script had just run into me at a club in Hollywood. In the looks department, he was a combination of Jim Morrison and Rick, my very first lay back on the beach in Florida. Mr. Writer was looking very hot in Helmut Lang jeans, a white T-shirt, and a red baseball cap, so I decided to hang out with him for a few days.

One night during this "hanging period," I brought my girlfriend Mary with me, for the sole purpose of showing her the guy I had designs on, so that when I started telling juicy stories about him later she'd have a visual.

Later that night, Mary and Mr. Writer got very drunk and he took her back to his hotel, where that ugly old baseball cap (not to mention other things) were neatly left in a pile in the middle of the floor while they fucked like rabbits.

Not only was my girlfriend having her way with the guy I'd been pursuing, but she had the balls to call me the next morning at 5:00 A.M., while I was getting ready to go on *Good Morning America*.

"Janice, I just want you to know that I didn't fuck him," she whispered—but her words were slightly slurred. It was clear that she was still jacked out of her gourd. Later that day I called him, and he was completely sober.

"What do you want me to do? Lie?" he retorted. "Of course I fucked her. She's a Scandy [short for the fabulous Scandinavian Viking goddesses who come to our country and take all of our men]." He said this like it was one of the basic facts of life: "Scandinavian model" equals "sleep with her, or lose your membership in the Men's Club of America." And he only dug himself in deeper when he mentioned he had *another* model girlfriend, whom he lived with in Brooklyn. *See, Janice? None of this really means anything.* To put a fine point on it, I hung up on him.

Cut to six months later, when Cap Boy called me again. "Hey, Janice, I'm in town tonight. Wanna hang?"

"My ass in your elbow, buddy!" I replied.

I might be a dumb model, but I'm not stupid. In fact, just telling you about this little betrayal reminds me of some other not-so-perfect sexual situations . . .

Take-It-Back Guys

Speaking of not-so-perfect sex, it's time to reacquaint ourselves with Sly Stallone. Whatever his performance in bed may have been, the guy knew how to give his partner great . . . gifts.

After our madcap dating escapade—and its oh-so-memorable sequel, when he demanded a DNA test to prove Savvy wasn't his child—Sly gave me the big heave-ho. Naturally, he demanded that the rather small diamond ring he had given me be sent back to him, immediately or sooner. Maybe it was my own pride, or the fact that the ring was butt-ugly, but I sent Rocky back his stupid rock, thinking that would be the end of his breakup demands.

Unfortunately, he wasn't quite finished. A few weeks after our breakup, Stallone sent some goon over to my house—or rather, he sent him *into* my house, with the key Sly had hung onto.

"Janice, I'm here for the stuff," said Goon Man, scaring the shit out of me as he walked into my living room and took two $500,000 paintings off the wall. It was like some bad episode of *The Sopranos.*

"Oh, I see Sly is a 'take it back' sort of guy," I replied without flinching.

"He wants the other rings," Goon insisted, taking out an actual list of goods he'd been sent to retrieve. At that point, I informed him of my motto: anyone who puts a ring on my finger had better be prepared to cut off the digit to get it back. My ex-husband Albert gave me a 23-karat ring, and it came in handy after we split—I lived off that thing for quite some time. Ladies, don't ever give the ring back. The least he can do is be a gentleman and let you keep a few door prizes.

Goon Boy walked into my kitchen like he expected to find the Hope Diamond in the fridge. *What the fuck is he looking for?* I thought, following him in. But I couldn't believe what I saw: his bug eyes were focused on my kitchen counter. Soon he was unplugging a twenty-two-dollar bagel toaster that Sly insisted I buy to warm up his bran muffins before his morning "training session."

"Don't you think Sylvester Stallone can afford to buy a new toaster?" I asked, but all he did was rip the cord out of the wall. A few sparks flew; the toaster was still warming up a bagel for my son. "Oh, you can have the food," said the Goon.

"I'm so thrilled," I retorted.

"I'm not done, Janice," he barked, swinging open my kitchen pantry and bending his fat ass down to haul out two cases of Diet Coke. Anyone who knows me learned a long time ago that the world's first supermodel has never indulged in diet drinks (too much sodium, and horrible for the skin). But Rambo loved to pop a few cans of diet chemicals on a hot day. "I know Sly's last few movies tanked, but I assume he can afford to replace his own carbonated beverages. Yes? No?" The Goon had no reply. The last time I checked, you could get those cases of Diet Coke for $4.99 on sale.

Now, minus some decent art, a shitty bagel toaster, and enough fizz to bloat a person for a month, I stood at the door as Sly's henchman peeled out of my driveway.

My God, what's next? I thought. *Maybe he'll come back for Sly's wrinkle cream.*

Ladies, this is why I'm not into prenups. Men want to take back the houses, the cars, the boats, sure—but they won't stop till they get the bagel burners. All I can say is, if you're ever paddling down this branch of Shit Creek, hang tough and remind your lawyer: *Once given, never taken back.*

Three Is the Loneliest Number

There are less-than-perfect sexual encounters on the Models' Love Ledger that would leave you reeling—even if it's been years since they happened. Take the time a certain Ms. X locked a model friend of mine—we'll call her Patricia—in a room at the Crillon Hotel in Paris for two straight days of nonstop sex with her and Mr. X. It was a two-day orgy, but it wasn't exactly Patricia's idea of a good time. In a way, she blames herself: there was more coke in that room than in any three charter flights out of Colombia, and she sampled the goods like everyone else was doing in those days.

All Patricia remembers was walking into that room in a red Valentino gown from a fashion awards dinner; a little snort, snort, snort; and before she knew it she was out of the dress, onto the bed, and totally at the mercy of Ms. X, the sex machine. Somehow Mr. X made his way into the room, and the two of them were fucking his big blond lights out. Patricia had to wait for both of them to literally pass out before she could make her getaway. It was a strange night, and as Patricia walked down the street in my—I mean *her*—red gown, she thought maybe she should stick to a different sort of threesome: she, herself, and her, alone in her own bed, just chilling out.

Bad Sex-a-Go-Go: Foreign Men Who Promise You the Freaking World

See, there was this head of state—I won't mention his name; I don't need any more men in black showing up at my door in the middle of the night. Well, I was doing a few print ads in his country, and one night he invited me to a restaurant with a name that began with Maison and ended with a $500 bill. I was compelled to say yes; after all, I was from the United States, proud of my heritage, and I thought my nation needed my services as a cultural ambassador.

After dinner, Mr. Powerful took me back to his penthouse suite at the best hotel in all the land. He dismissed the armed guards, double-locked the doors, took off his bulletproof vest, and turned down the lights.

But he couldn't get it up.

It was a little disappointing. Here I was, already fancying myself a rock 'n' roll Princess Grace. I knew I'd look damn good in one of those little diamond tiaras—and besides, I've always wanted a moat.

"Jan-eese!" my foreign billionaire moaned, trying to seal the deal some other other way. "I can give you a fur coat, a Ferrari, a parcel of land in the South of France. *Anything* if you would be my mistress."

As much as I liked the idea of owning some French countryside, I just had to say no, though. What me and my big trap actually said: "Are you kidding me? I don't think so. You need to, uh, be able to fly a different type of flag in order to keep my interest."

The only thing I walked away with that night was a pound of caviar from the minibar and the little gold crest off his jacket.

Pointing Fingers at the Polish Prince of a Proctologist

Another day, another foreigner.

Every now and then I'll break some of my own cardinal rules—I will slip up and let a man take control of my emotions. (Temporary insanity kicks in until I regain the title.) So one night I caved and slept with this incredibly handsome, big-shouldered, square-jawed, dark-haired Polish proctologist. He was also a billionaire businessman who had the longest uncircumcised member I'd ever seen. In other words, he was a total foreign hottie. The sex was amazing, thanks to the fact that his parents didn't believe in that little nip-and-tuck at birth. I left smiling—but also wondering why I'd allowed him to bring me to his home. And why did I put up with him smoking those hideous hand-rolled cigarettes that made me want to barf the minute he lit up?

I should have been hanging out in the back of Prince's limousine.

And the biggest question of all: Could I stand going to Poland on vacation?

Fuck! I actually had the hots for the guy, which is always the worst possible scenario. That's when men have the power to hurt you.

Case in point: The next day, I waited and waited for the Polish prince to call me. We'd loosely made plans to team up at a *Self* magazine dinner, but by noon he hadn't called to firm things up (so to speak), and I was so jumpy and livid that I sent him an e-mail saying that our plans were on hold because the magazine wanted me to walk in with Josh Hartnett.

By three that afternoon, something totally shocking happened, and it wasn't Hartnett pulling up in my driveway in a Mercedes. Mr. Poland still hadn't called.

Ladies, I want you to know that sometimes even I have to remind myself of a simple fact: Men will mess with your mind if you let them. This was a perfect time to enroll myself in . . . yes, you guessed it: My School of Discipline. I called a few girlfriends, had a workout and a manicure, took in an AA meeting, went shopping, and sent myself some flowers. (*Who knows?* I thought. *They might come in handy later.*)

I also got out my best, shortest, hottest beige Diane von Furstenberg minidress and gold-strappy Gucci stilettos. The leader of Clan Female (*moi*) was all set to go to the event solo. Screw him! Ultra-egomaniac supermodel that I am, I cursed him out repeatedly as I groomed myself for the evening. Still, one part of me was caught up in wondering how he could possibly leave me hanging after all that great sex.

And just when I'd whined enough about all this on my cell phone, the phone rang. It was Mr. Poland, apologizing profusely: he'd been in meetings all day, and was running late, but he'd be there ASAP.

Be still my heart.

At the end of the evening, after the caviar, after all the air kisses and asskissing, and finally after a few suggestive slow dances with Mr. Poland, our limo rolled up to my driveway. I'm sure he expected to be invited in to share some Polish sausage, but I just kissed him politely on the cheek. "I've got an early call tomorrow."

As he watched me sashay into my house like I was walking a New York runway, he looked like he could barely speak. *My, my, my,* how good this felt. For once it wasn't my dog Bruno panting in the house—it was the dog outside who was salivating, maybe even licking his own balls. (It sure wasn't going to be me doing the honors!)

Oh, in the interest of future peace with Poland, let me reassure you all—yes, he called six times the next day. Sad but true: as we've seen time and again, feigning lack of interest is the oldest and most perfect trick in the book. Holding back works every time.

That said, it's no guarantee that they won't pull the same shit the next time they get a chance.

A few weeks later, on a chilly winter night in Hollywood, I had another date with the ol' Pole. Five minutes before six, though, I still hadn't heard from him. So there I was sitting in my Mercedes across the street from the Peninsula Hotel, waiting to go down the red carpet for a magazine launch he was supposed to attend as my date. I was all alone in a sea of fake tits and lifted asses, looking hot in my tight Frankie B jeans, and burning mad.

So I decided to call this late bastard and give him a piece of my mind. Of course, I got his answering machine, which would have to do. Doing my best to conjure up a voice that could turn water into ice, I said, "Who the fuck do you think you are? I'm used to being treated like a queen. And by the way, you will no longer be boinking this queen. So off with your head—and lose my number. The thrill is gone, honey. Janice Dickinson doesn't get stood up."

A few minutes later, my cell rang. Unluckily for him, I was still sitting in my car, fuming away.

"Janice, I was waiting for you to call me all day long. I thought you were standing *me* up this time," he insisted.

How could I deport this guy?

"I've been in meetings all day long," he went on. "But my suit's in the back of my car. I was waiting for you."

Shit. I hate when guys try the Freudian turn-it-around trick. Suddenly it's all *your* fault, and they're just moronic pups sitting there waiting to be told what to do.

"Look, I haven't just been around the block," I told him. "I've been around the town. That excuse of yours was invented in 1947. It might have worked for Cary Grant, but honey, you're no Cary Grant." I would have smashed my cell phone right then and there if I didn't need it to survive.

Was that enough? Don't know the meaning of the word. Can a woman ever own enough black or expensive shoes? "Josh Hartnett's publicist just called my publicist to see if we could attend this thing together, but I had to say, 'No, I'm waiting for this Polish proctologist.'" After using the word "fuck" three times in one sentence, I hung up on him.

The latest victim of My School of Discipline, he called me all night long. And in his last call he was still pleading for me to call him back. In Poland, he claimed, the girl would have called *him* to confirm plans. "Janice, I was waiting for you to tell me where and when," he pleaded again. "I'm a doctor. I have things to do. I have people with proctologic emergencies." (For once, I didn't want any details.)

"For a doctor, you sure have a lousy bedside manner," I retorted. "Plus, if you're so busy that you don't have time for me, you can forget it!"

The next morning it started all over again. "Janice, what do I have to do to get back into your good graces?" he said, a new level of desperation creeping into his voice.

Hmm. Think on your feet, Janice. "I'll see you in Bali this weekend," I told him. "It's on you. I'll be waiting for you to send me a first-class ticket," I said. Later that weekend, the Pole told me, "You going off on me like that made me like you so much more. It was just so passionate. You American girls have such fire."

Oh, if he wanted a little fire, I could certainly light the match.

"I need a new Rolex for the trip," I told him over dinner before the trip, and he immediately took out a credit card and drove to Harry Winston's. Meanwhile, two tan businessmen passed me in the diamond earring aisle and gave me the head-to-toe once-over, which made the Pole turn red with rage. (No big challenge for Mr. Euro-pasty.)

But I wasn't ready to welcome Poland back into the world community—not just yet. So I checked out the asses of the businessmen in front of him. "Would you like a necklace to go with your watch?" my date inquired.

"No, I don't need a necklace. But that ruby bracelet might be nice."

Ka-ching.

15

Advanced Faking It
for Men

Most women wonder about their FQ on a daily basis. *Fuckability quotient,* that is. Even the world's first supermodel knows it ain't always happening, for one very simple reason: maintenance, maintenance, maintenance.

I listen to women complain about their bodies—and I usually think they're right. After all, would you drive a Ferrari with threadbare wheels and scratched rims? Yet on a daily basis I go to Maha Yoga in swanky Brentwood and stare, not into the souls but at the *soles* of some of the richest and most fantastic bitches on this planet. It makes me want to puke: 99.9 percent of these women have feet that look like they're covered in old alligator skin. I know it's not very Zen of me to say so, but haven't these women heard about pumicing, salt and sugar scrubs, and the mysteries of bag bum wraps?

When I'm not out on the town, I spend my nights slathering my feet with moisturizer, then covering the whole concoction with white socks to help it all soak in. To complete the package, I put collagen patches under

my eyes and rubber gloves filled with moisturizer on my hands, so it all just melts into my fingers like butter into a roll.

By this point, of course, actual in-person sex is out of the question. My *dogs* don't even want to be near me. I'm so greasy at this point, lingerie isn't even an option. Instead, I hop into my flannel pajamas. FQ: Off-the-charts low.

At moments like this, there's only one option to keep your man entertained: phone sex.

A word of caution, though: Be *very* careful. You may think no one can see you as you conjure up a verbal *Playboy* spread in your lover's mind's eye. As with anything else, though, there are hidden dangers around every corner.

Take the story of my friend and fellow model Kelly LeBrock, of *The Woman in Red* film fame. Back in the A-list days, when she was married to Steven Segal, the two of them relied on nightly phone sex to carry them through the lonely times.

One night, these two poor babies were "missing each other terribly." He was stuck on some movie set in Canada, and Kelly was pining away in their Beverly Hills home.

Steven: "Baby, what are you wearing?"

Kelly: "Oh, it's this incredible La Perla lingerie from Paris. I'm touching it right now and it's silky . . . and now I'm moving up to satin and lace. I have a salmon-pink thong next to my silky skin, Stevie."

Poor Kel was so into it she didn't hear the door of the bedroom click open. Luckily it wasn't a burglar—but it was Segal, holding one of those huge cell phones from back in the day that stretched from your elbow to your hand. Ponytail flipping, he strode in expecting that pink salmon thong. WRONG-O! There was my friend Kelly in total maintenance mode, rocking three layers of sweatpants and enough thick moisturizer to spackle a wall with her cheekbones.

Opposite: German *Playboy* self-portrait. Love that phone!

Point of the story: If you're having phone sex while dressed like a slob, make sure the guy isn't within driving distance—or his little fantasy could get deflated right quick.

As for me, I don't give that many specifics during phone sex.

Hot guy to Janice: "Baby, what are you wearing?"

Me: "Chanel Number Five."

(Thank you, Marilyn Monroe.)

Even in my bag bums, I'm still telling the truth.

In the end, what should we do with men? It's an impossible question.

And now it's getting even more complicated. Because now I'm having to teach my daughter, Savvy, all about the male species.

She was with me the other day when Evan Marriott (the first Joe Millionaire—remember?) cruised by and gave me the slow once-over while we were walking down Rodeo Drive. So naturally I turned around and grabbed a look at Joe's ass, which wasn't really all that hot compared to some other contenders I'd seen walking down that street.

With his $500,000 check, of course, Joe was only half a millionaire—and that was before taxes. I wasn't so sure I liked his attitude, not to mention all that lying he did in the name of prime-time ratings. "Savvy, you see Joe Millionaire over there?" I asked. My ten-year-old seemed rather uninterested. Still, I knew it was my job as her mother to impart a bit of wisdom she could carry with her the rest of her life. "You don't give men like that the time of day. You do exactly what I'm about to do now—*keep walking.*

"And never look back. It's the looking back that gets you in trouble," I added.

My sweet daughter just looked up at me and rolled her eyes. She's ten going on forty, and it worries the hell out of me. Know what I mean?

I'm not letting her go out with a man until I'm in the grave.

PART III
LOOKS AND BEAUTY

The other day, I was climbing out of the bathtub when my eyes caught my reflection in the mirror. My big lovely tits, I suddenly noticed, weren't quite what they used to be. I thought, *If I can't have another kid, then maybe I should at least buy myself a new pair of tits. I mean, Christ, I deserve a little something, right?*

Society has a strange reaction to women who strive to better themselves in every way possible. We're labeled "high-maintenance," which is a term I've never quite understood. What's the idea—you're supposed to take care of yourself in every way as a woman, pretending all along that it's all just second nature? When is it that you're supposed to get all your precious beauty chores done—in the middle of the night, when no one's looking? Ridiculous!

As you can imagine, I'm especially amused by men who say they want a "low-maintenance girlfriend." There's a shortsighted collection of individuals. The minute Mr. I Love LM invites a girl to the beach—and finds her standing there in a bikini with pubic hair as thick as the shrubs on her front lawn—what do you think he's going to say, "I love this bitch—she's so LM!"? *Please.*

Here's what he's going to say: "What the hell is *that?* Come back when you've invested in a Weed Whacker."

If your guy tells you you're too HM, there's only one way to save your relationship: *Forget about that relationship.* Start looking for another guy. If he bitches about the hour you spend in the bathroom, don't even waste your breath responding. You're doing it for *you*, after all, not for him. That's the true bottom line when it comes to your own personal beauty plan—supermodel or superwoman.

The bottom line is, it costs time, bucks, and pain to be perfect. It costs dough to hire those Brazilian waxers to hack away the shrubbery. It costs to have your feet scraped, descaled, chiseled, and polished so they'll look good in a pair of Jimmy Choos. It costs to have those fake Mystic Tans sprayed on our hides, so we can be healthy now without spending our Golden Years swigging chemo drugs. It costs to exfoliate, sand, grind, tuck, and squeeze. It's endless.

Hell, it even costs to buy all the magazines every month: *Vogue, Allure, Cosmo, Glamour,* and *Mademoiselle.* I just tell myself the magazines weigh as much as dictionaries—just picking them up must give me a little workout.

Am I high-maintenance just because I have my hair triple-processed? I pay through my perfectly capped teeth for down 'dos, straight 'dos, under 'dos, and up 'dos. I just tell myself I'm mixing things up.

But I'm lucky: no one has ever dared to call Janice high-maintenance—not to my face, anyway. My motto is: *Move over and let the Big Dog eat.* When my fangs are out and I'm prepping, no one dares question the process.

So let's get *you* prepped—starting right now. Just follow these simple and cheap beauty tips and—well, *beware!* You'll be *on fire!*

It's perfectly doable. Just read on.

16.

The Perfect Body Image: Fat or Phat?

In 2003, *Vogue* did a body shape issue celebrating every size, from 0 through 20. Friends called me and said, "Janice, do you think bigger can be better? Can fatter be sexier?" I have to admit I thought some of the girls looked pretty damn chunky—but to each her own. I was never able to celebrate an extra pound—heaven forbid ten! Then again, that's also why I starved myself to death for the better part of two decades.

How nuts can you get with a diet? Well, the other day I was actually thinking celery was a pretty tasty afternoon snack. What a wonderful imagination I have.

The Big and the Not-So-Beautiful

At the age of forty-seven, I'm lucky: I can still drop my clothes without needing therapy, and I still do fashion shoots in bathing suits the size of dental floss. I'm not saying this to show off; I mention it because I work hard almost every single day of my life to look this way. I could look at it

**Du bleu
pour deux**

A gauche, T-shirt
maille viscose e
short en crêpe d
laine (les deux
Christian Lacroi
Pour la petite fil
maillot de bai
(Souleïado).

**Trio tendres
à Santa Mon**

A droite, robe
maille de lain
empiècemen
rebrodé de per
et veste en cote
gansé (Sonia
Rykiel).

Les enfants port
des T-shirts en co
peigné (Armor L
● Pour les adres
reportez-vous p
ou, pour tout au
renseignemen
téléphonez
au 36 68 87

Maquillage
Thierry Maud
pour Rochas
Coiffures
John Birchall

Photos réalisé
à Los Angele
Avec nos
remerciements
Beverly Hills H

Réalisation
Joseph Carl

as part of my job, but I actually think of this work as a way to keep me sane. I'm one of the strange ones. I love to get out there and sweat. It feels good, even when I'm literally sweating out my stress while working on my body. I feel fit, strong, and healthy. What's wrong with all of the above?

Yet there's a strange thing happening in the modeling industry. I've been hearing that a new breed of women will soon be squashing women like me. They're calling themselves plus-size models—the "big girls."

The fact is, I don't buy this new attempt to shove their supersize images down our throats. When women ten sizes overweight are crawling all over the fashion mags, what have we come to?

Women like Missy Elliott and Queen Latifah are in *Vogue*—in fact, they're taking over the glossy pages. Recently I read an article about their eating secrets, and I almost had a stroke. Truth Squad: I don't think what they're eating is actually such a big secret. Who doesn't know how to get ahold of a couple bags of chocolate-chip cookies?

I'm all for stroking the egos of our plus-size friends, but I'd also like some of them to move into my house for a month. First of all, Queen Latifah looks like a lot of fun, and I'm sure we'd get down. She could teach me how to sing, and I'd have her cutting out carbs and doing yoga. As for Mademoiselle Elliott, I'd say, "Missy, put down that muffin, and join your sista Janice in a little walk around the canyon. We'll make fun of all the other bitches and hos on the trail." Man, if that isn't a fun morning out, then I don't know what is.

I'll give Carré Otis a pass for her recent coming-out as a bigger girl. I understand Carré's plight better than anyone: she was eating carrots as a main course (like me) throughout the 1980s. She could swallow one peanut and call it dessert. Carré has a perfect face, and the camera loves that puss. She also must have residual issues from all those years with the "complicated" actor Mickey Rourke. I mean, you'd pick up a gallon of Rocky Road, too, if you had to deal with his shit.

Opposite: Personal fave. No sleep the night before due to the departure of a marriage.

But *Emme?* They should seal her lips together.

Anna Nicole Smith, in my book, is a pig. I'm not sure where her tits end and her stomach rolls begin. When I saw her drinking wine on an episode of her E! series, I began to understand: she doesn't sip, she guzzles. Ugh! How many grapes had to die for that woman to get a buzz on?

On the other hand, Anna was smart enough to marry that shriveled-up billionaire—and to convince a court of law that their relationship was "true love," topped off with sizzling sex. *Voilà!* Now she's a zillionaire. Here's hoping he left this earth with a smile on his face from watching Anna suck on . . . all that wine.

Maybe I should give Anna another shot after all. She might be a pig, but she's a very smart girl when it comes to scoping out fiscal opportunity. Anna, if you're reading this, the world's first supermodel says you can call anytime to talk about business ventures. Just please put a bra on—all that flesh makes me want to get lipo, darling.

17.

Toning Up Body and Mind— In a Hurry

I wake up every morning like a racehorse, fueled by adrenaline. I'm not sure where it comes from, but I thank God it's there. Still, I've still got a devil on my shoulder who's looking to send that horse to the glue factory. Every morning I fight that little voice that tells me, *You don't have to do anything today. Rest on your laurels—hell, rest on your fat ass.* I just throw cold water on that feeling the minute I step into the shower.

Once I'm conscious, though, things get a little bit tricky because then all the self-doubt kicks in. Many women, including myself, go through life thinking, *What do I need to change about myself? It's too much, so forget it.* So how do you do it? Take a deep breath and I'll help you. I mean it. All you have to do to start is close your eyes and inhale.

Even before I open my eyes in the morning, I begin by doing something known as navel yoga. It's basically a half hour of deep, slow breathing exercises that primarily tone the stomach. Mine, as a result, is like a rock.

With all this heavy breathing, I know I may sound like a dog in heat or a phone prankster. But I don't care—it works. I also meditate while I breathe, which is something I've been doing for more than two decades. I got initiated into the art of meditation twenty-five years ago at the Meditation Center in New York: they taught me how to sit down, breathe in, breathe out, and focus on a mantra they give you.

Every morning, for twenty to thirty minutes, I follow this deep breathing with some simple stretches. This combo platter of breathing and stretching gets me off to the right start—it helps me bring out the power in me before life (jobs, kids, men) tries to suck me dry. Then, just in case I'm not feeling 100 percent when I'm done, I'll whip out some positive affirmations. This is not just some selfish, stupid bullshit, no matter what anyone says. Try starting your morning by saying the following: "I affirm that I will prevail during this day—prevail and sail on."

I promise you this: if I didn't do everything I just described (and what I'm getting to in a minute), I'd lose my mind. I wouldn't have the career, or the children, or the boyfriend, or the work, or the new TV show. I would never be able to do it without this routine.

But I'm not done yet. Cut to SHOWER SCENE: **Janice Dickinson**, naked, lathering myself with the most wonderful bath products. My personal favorite right now is the St. Ives Vanilla Swiss with Vitamin E body wash. I love the smell of vanilla; it just plain makes me happy. And when I'm inching toward truly feeling good in the shower, I do something that just tips things right over the edge: I raise one clean, soon-to-be-moisturized arm up proud in the air, just like the Statue of Liberty. Remember, I was raised in the 1960s; *power to the people!* still means something to me. At that moment at the beginning of each new day, when I raise my fist in the air, I feel my own power.

Tick-tock, tick-tock. My brain's internal clock is always ticking away, and my God, it's running fast. I'm always in a hurry, especially when it comes to toning up my bod or my mind. We've already discussed the breathing, meditation, and affirmation process. Often, I follow it all with a nice hike and a prayer. In other words, a workout plan for body *and* soul. If I don't do all five—breathe, think, reaffirm, hike, pray—then I'm in deep shit.

I follow this up by sitting down for a few minutes and writing my feelings down on a piece of paper. Some days, my notebook reads about like this: "I'm a lost cause. I'm a downer. I'm not good enough—not good for my children, not good for society." Those are the bad days. If the cops in L.A. could write tickets for feelings, I'd be booked as a "negligent operator."

Why does my head fill up with these negative thoughts? Oh, I don't know: frustration, anguish, pent-up rage, low self-esteem. But there's good news: I don't feel that way every single day anymore. This doesn't mean my mind still doesn't host a bad thought from time to time, even when I'm trying to calm myself down. I'm so hyper that even during the most relaxing part of life, which is yoga class, I can't slow down. It turns out

A MAHA Yogatini (right). Really just trying to get the rust out.

that yoga has been a pretty fast way to tone up, which for a speed demon like me is a very good thing.

Yoga has been a part of my life since I was fourteen. My father did one decent thing I know of in his life: he happened to bring home a book from the Far East filled with yoga positions. One night when he wasn't looking, I snuck the book up to my room and became obsessed with trying out every single position I could manage. The agonizing hours I'd spent trying to be a ballet dancer had left me surprisingly limber, and yoga just came easily. A few months later, I read an article about a man from California named Bikram who had his own take on yoga. I began to search for books by him, and I copied all of his positions, too. I've never looked back.

The bottom line is, yoga works. It helps you fight gravity because half the positions have you upside down. It's good for arthritis, high blood pressure, spider veins, varicose veins, fat thighs, and your sex life; it can even help you pop out babies without as much pain. You've got to love a discipline that has an exercise called "breath of fire." (No, it has nothing to do with spicy food.) The breath of fire keeps your abdomen flat, flat, flat! I do them backward, to help flatten out anything that dares to protrude from my belly. With the breath of fire, what firms up *stays* firm, too.

When I go to yoga classes, I stride in with a look that says, *I know what I'm doing.* Ladies, that's half the battle right there. To the average layperson, I'm a freaking yoga expert. My head may tell me otherwise, but only my head and I know the truth. The minute I roll out my purple yoga mat and go through a series of stretches, silence falls over the room. Suddenly a powerful groan emerges from somewhere within me, and a gaggle of giggles pours out. The class ends with a loud "*om*"—and mine is always the loudest.

Yoga, to me, is holy. I love the sounds of silence when I'm doing a "downward dog." For a few moments, I'm so wrapped and tangled up that I forget to hate myself; sometimes I even manage to forgive myself for everything—past, present, and future.

Why not try the same yourself? If you need a motivation, find one. Find the button that lights up the *Go, go, go!* sign in your brain, and push it. Maybe you need to relax. Maybe you need to forgive yourself, too. Maybe you just want to be able to look down and see your nicest pair of shoes without your gut getting in the way. Whatever it is, find it and *get moving*. Stop leaning over to find your feet, move your ass, and *do it!*

Even before I have my morning coffee, I try to do something physical. Walking uphill is key. I'm not a runner; bless you if you can move your groove thing at top speed, but that's simply not me. I don't even do that career-girl power walk, where your arms swing out like you're about to merge two Fortune 500 companies. I just find hills and walk up them at a reasonable rate of speed. It'll keep the ass off the back of your knees. I promise.

Even if your ass has been hanging longer than the Mona Lisa, you can fix it. Just get out there and walk on an incline. Walk, walk, walk, walk. If you think it'll help you, you can always buy yourself a walking tape—or choose your own music, like I do.

You can walk with a girlfriend; I hear it can work, but I don't like to exercise with anyone except my two dogs. The only *people* I actually like to walk with are my kids, but they've stopped exercising with Mom, and I don't push it because God knows I don't want them to develop some kind of complex over hanging out in public with their hot mama. I've even tried walking with boyfriends—but in my experience, anyway, most men are better oglers than they are walkers.

If you live in a shitty climate, there's always treadmill walking. But you *must* set that machine on an incline. (Yes, you do. Don't argue with me. I don't care what your trainer's been telling you. Ever consider that he likes you plump because it means return business?) Walking on an incline is the only way to repair and reshape that ass. And when the ass in question starts screaming from the 3.0 incline, just say these words: "In a few months, I'll buy a pair of stretchy Dolce & Gabbana jeans." It makes the ache worth it, so slap that puppy on an incline.

As for the rest of the exercises: yes, there are thousands of books out there, and even more tapes from models, actresses, and their trainers. I've never tried any of them. I just do the simple program that I've outlined above. I walk and do yoga. It's worked for me for almost four decades.

At the end of the day, though, it's *you* who must take the initiative. It doesn't matter whether you're the solitary type, or do it with your best girlfriend, or join a running group: you're the only one who can wake up in the morning and scream, *Yeeeeeaaahhh! I'm going out again today.* You owe it to yourself.

At certain times in my life, I've been forced to supplement all this with more drastic measures. When I had Nathan I was only thirty-two, and I was still hot on the modeling circuit; I had to do something to get

Perfect jeans. Perfect ass. Loving myself a bit too much here.

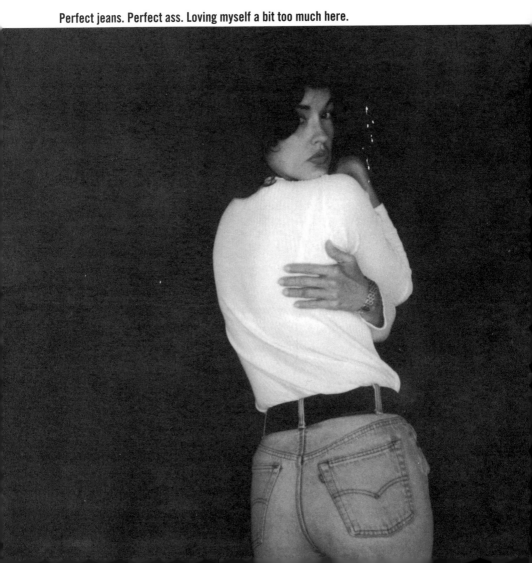

back into top shape right away. So I started incorporating *serious* uphill walking into my training. From time to time I got other ideas: when I was carrying all that postnatal baby weight, I'll admit it occurred to me that I could start losing by just buying a pound of blow and going on the Drug Addict Diet. But I knew I couldn't do that and take care of this young child. So I started walking up those hills, and the weight began to fall off my ass. The more I walked, the more I lost. I was always a walker when I lived in New York. I've got an active imagination, and every day I'd go outside and imagine I was walking in the south of France. I've always had a lot of Walter Mitty characters floating around my brain. It helps to pass the time.

So is my body perfect today? *Come on.* I've had two children, and I eat a bit of sugar, so my rock-hard stomach muscles are sheathed in a slender little layer of baby fat. It's been a while since I've had zero body fat, but I still dream of it, which gets me closer to my goal.

Of course, my favorite form of exercise is very basic—riding on top. (Sorry, kids—no photos.)

Now let's talk about cellulite for a second. Last year, those bastards at the tabloids ran a photo of Jennifer Lopez with her skirt hiked up to her privates. It wasn't so much that they wanted to sneak a peek at the goods. What their inquiring minds *really* wanted to expose was a patch of cottage cheese–like cellulite that was supposedly dimpling her otherwise very toned thighs. I'll admit it: I took a gander at J.Lo's supposed imperfections, and even indulged in a moment of glee at the expense of another international sex symbol. *My, my. I guess Jerry Hall isn't the only one with thighs like sheets of sandpaper.*

As soon as I thought it, though, I felt a little guilty—or maybe just taken for a little ride. Why? Because as a public person I know the drill when it comes to those trashy mags. The next time you're feeling smug while checking out their newest "exclusive photos" of some superstar's less-than-super body, ask yourself how easy it would have been for them to add a little digital fat to her famous person's arms, legs, or rump. It's a dirty thing for the tabloids to do because I'm guessing that most celebs work their asses off to look good. I know I see J.Lo on the path I hike on the Franklin Canyon outside of Los Angeles. I don't think the woman could possibly have much cellulite on her because her trainer, Gunner Peterson, works her like a dog. She's intense, fast, and serious when it comes to training. So take that, you greasy tabloid. (This is the same so-called magazine that once sent a reporter to stand outside my home digging through the trash to find "good garbage." I hope they found some good used tampons.)

Tabloids: therein lies the downside of being famous. They printed that I used Sly Stallone, falsely pretending that he was my daughter's father. *Not true.* They printed that I sued him for child support. *Also not true.*

But if I ever catch sight of cellulite and me in the same photograph—well, you know someone's going down.

18.

Extreme Model Makeover (aka Janice Goes Under the Knife!)

The other day I saw a bulldog walking down Rodeo Drive, and one single thought went through my mind: *Boy, that character needs about twenty shots of Botox.* When you start thinking about how you can fix canines, it's a definite sign that you've gone too far in your quest for perfection. (Of course, the same thing happened when I looked up at the dog's master. You know how they always say that dogs and their owners look alike? Here was a case where they could both have used a nice pull from a good surgeon.)

I will go to any extent to suffer for beauty. That's just who I am. If I could get to the moon, grab a few rocks, and rub them on my skin to exfoliate, well, I'd do it. I'm willing to do anything to help maintain my youthfulness. And the only difference between me and all the other women running around the greater Los Angeles area is that I'm not afraid to admit it.

I'm not alone in my quest for youthful perfection. Name a star, and I'll point out the work that she or he has had done. Little-known fact:

Marilyn Monroe was born with six toes. She had a surgeon whack one off so she'd look good in heels. Elvis Presley and Dean Martin both had nose jobs. And there are plenty of other examples from the present day. I can't provide you with diagrams—I've got lawyers reading this book, after all—but think about it: how many thirty-year-olds do you know whose face looks as good as most of the fifty-year-olds on the big screen?

Of course, the point is that we *don't* think about it. We the gullible public—and this means us especially, ladies—have been duped into thinking most of the actresses and models working today just waltzed out of bed looking absolutely stunning. Just think about it: we're talking decades of gravitational pull, a handful of bad marriages, and about a thousand pounds of makeup per babe. There isn't a woman out there who could be dewy-fresh after all of the above, and those who say that they "don't believe in surgery"—well, they're full of shit.

I hate it when the average woman says to me, "Janice, I try and try to look like [favorite celebrity here]. I do the workout regime she outlined first in *Sassy* and later in *More*. But my hips still have dimples, and my ass is still pointing south. My chin is sagging, and those little wrinkles around my eyes don't seem to go away, no matter how hard I try 'living the simple life.'"

Sure, the celebs of the hour might be working out in the gym six times a week, but they're also going under the knife. In Hollywood, people schedule plastic surgeries like they're making dinner reservations. *Hello, yes, I need a quiet spot to rest and a set of new tits. Thursday? Seven a.m.? I'll be there. You bring the saline, I'll bring the plastic.*

I'm no different. It's funny, but the first time I set foot in a plastic surgeon's office, back in 1989, had exactly nothing to do with wanting to look twenty. My only trouble was that my *foot* was killing me. As anyone who's ever had a painful bunion will tell you, that kind of pain is enough to make you want to grab a gun and shoot yourself. Of course, beauty was the reason I was in this pain. It all reverts back to the B-word. In the interest of

Opposite: Should I jump? Nah, I look too good.

glamour, I'd spent years with my feet pinched, squeezed, and crammed into the highest shoes I could direct up and down a runway. Honestly, the only thing I didn't subject my feet to was binding them like a Kabuki princess.

My bun-ectomy was as painful as it sounds. But as I recovered from a painful infection, I began mulling over other ideas: *If I can withstand just a little more pain, who knows how many other things I could fix?* Armed with a big bottle of extra-strength Tylenol, I sorted through a mental catalog of Janice's "could use a little assistance." Suddenly there seemed to be nothing that a good doctor with a sharp scalpel and a clever payment plan couldn't help me fix.

My tits were the obvious next stop. After I had Nathan, I noticed (much to my shock) that my boobs had deflated into two soggy pancakes. Knowing I had to pump up the volume, I enlisted the help of a great plastic surgeon. So the first time I had 'em done, it was a gift to myself. It was a gift the second time, too—courtesy of Sly Stallone, the Great Tit Fairy. Sly passed out new boobs like they were welcome gifts, just for hanging out with him. I accepted his hospitality.

Around that time, I also decided to expand my horizons: I had my eyelids done and my face pinched back. In many ways, having this kind of work done feels like redecorating your house: you buy a new couch, and then the carpeting looks like shit. So you rip *that* up, and then you have to put in new fixtures. It never ends. (Hell, I'd have a penile implant if they'd let me. At times I've been both mother and father to both of my children, so why not rock the dual equipment?)

When I went on Dr. Phil's show last year (primarily to hawk books, let's be honest), he looked at me with great disdain the minute the cameras went live. When I told him I was addicted to plastic surgery, he reacted as if it were his biggest eureka moment of the week. He stared

Opposite: Taking advantage of my time alone in an unnamed New York City hotel suite.

deeply at me, as if he were expecting me to burst into tears and hug him for "getting to the bottom of me."

I just sighed. I was there to share beauty tips and books ("Please buy one!") with the masses; now this guy was trying to be my own personal daytime savior.

What was so strange about all this was that the day before the show, the pre-interview I'd done with one of Dr. Phil's staff went very differently. One gal—who seemed to be about twenty years old—asked me all about my breast surgeries and lipo. She wanted some of both *and ASAP*, thank you very much. I tried to tell her that it was up to the individual to decide what was best for her. I also told her that I invented the fuck-me pose, both before and after surgery. In other words, it's all about *attitude*, not bra size.

But there was Dr. Phil, standing in front of his fawning studio audience, ripping me a new one. He made it seem like all I ever did with my life was sign up for another session under the knife. Between his comments, I tried to explain to him and his audience how much more there was to the story: how most models are digitally enhanced in magazines; how many wear those little chicken-cutlet-looking breast-enhancing inserts. *This* is the kind of information women need to know, so they won't want to kill themselves just because they don't look like they just jumped off the glossy pages of *Cosmo*.

But Dr. Phil wasn't interested in helping me inspire women, helping me show them how to come to peace with their own bodies. All he wanted to hear was how everything about me was fake: fake teeth, fake tits, fake hair, eye and foot work, and so forth. "I'm considering an ass lift," I joked. "What's wrong with a little insurance against the earth's gravitational pull?"

Phil looked like he might drop over. "I'm addicted to looking good," I told him. "I used to be addicted to alcohol, coke, prescription pills, and sex." Pause. "I'm still a passion addict, but I also like to clean the house every single day. I just do everything to the extreme."

Well, Phil was not convinced. "My objective here is to share," I said.

Knowing that trying to appeal to him would be a losing battle, I looked into the audience and said, "Ladies, anyone here ever have bunion problems? Would you like to get that thing on your foot whacked off? Well, don't do it because soon you'll have new tits." The cheers were so deafening I thought I was at a Stones concert.

"Janice, perhaps your multiple surgeries are just a cry for help. You're trying to fill yourself and fix yourself artificially," Dr. Phil went on. When I looked totally bored with that approach, he switched tactics.

"What do you think we should do here, young lady?" Dr. Phil asked me.

Dr. Phil asking *me* for guidance? Now that's more like it. Phil, baby, turn back to page one and start reading from the beginning. When it comes to giving other people advice—even the reigning king of self-help—I'm full of ideas.

19.
In the Butt, Bob

It doesn't matter if he's a horn dog, a big brain, a Wall Street bore, or a road warrior. The first thing a guy looks for in a woman is a nice ass. Call me a freak (I am), but the ass is our national treasure, girls.

Let me tell you a little story. One night I was at On the Roxx, a hot L.A. club, gyrating all by myself. Of course, Mr. Mick Jagger (is he stalking me?) pranced up to me, looked down at my basic fuck-me pumps and fishnets (with seams, of course), and then slowly gazed up at my micromini. His eyes went *boiiiiing* when he got to the ass. *Hello, Betty!*

That's how you get your man—gay, straight, or anywhere in between. Thanks to Marc Jacobs and his stiletto pumps, my ass looked just right. Mick just said, "Hello, remember me?" The rest was history.

Moral of the story: it's not about boobs. It's not about the face, the smile, or the eyes. It's about the ass. It's *la derrière* in French. In Italian it's the *coo'*. You get the idea. The ass is the international symbol of sex appeal. Asses translate. They transcend all time zones and geographical borders.

Here are some great (and not-so-great) asses from the movies:

Mel Gibson: Put his butt near the barbie and turn around, mate!

Brad Pitt: Yes, yes, yes. Meet Joe Butt.

Richard Gere: Classic back end, and all that jazz.

Tyrese: What's up, baby boy?

George Clooney: Funny guy, flat ass, move on. (Sorry, George, I had to reevaluate after seeing your last movie.)

And this didn't all happen overnight. Now let's rewind to a momentous time in television history. Time: 1977. Place: Burbank, California. Show: *The Newlywed Game*. Bob Eubanks asked a suburban wife, "What's the weirdest place you've ever gotten the urge to make whoopee?"

Blushing Betty to Bob: "Is it in the butt, Bob?"

Ain't it the truth?

Today, of course, everyone's on the same page as Betty. J.Lo's Rump Revolution put it into the mainstream. At the risk of getting my own ass kicked, though, I *would* say she's got a pretty wide load. Baby got back— but it's just not my kind of butt.

Now, Gisele Bundchen, *she's* got it back there. So, for that matter, does any prima ballerina, from the American Ballet Company on down. They're my ideal girls with great asses. I have a picture of one of those dancers on my fridge, with a little note I wrote myself to stop myself in my tracks when I've got the munchies: *Look at those butts. Now, don't open that door!*

I'll tell it to you straight: Half my commitment to working out stems from my own fears of losing my posterior power. That's why I walked ten miles a day at the right pace when I was back in New York working on *America's Next Top Model*. That's why I get up at five-thirty every morning and walk up a canyon in Los Angeles. Yeah, it's good for your heart, but it's even better for your assets.

20.

Dressed to Maim

This chapter is dedicated to one of my role models: Miss Winona Ryder. Honey, I understand your need to shop, shop, shop until you drop—even if it results in a pesky court case. Never you mind those prying eyes at Saks Fifth Avenue. I feel your pain.

You see, I'm the victim of shopping "blackouts" myself. And it's not my fault. I'm a shopping *fiend*. On any given day, I'll find bags in my closet, and it's like a reverse robbery has happened at my Beverly Hills home. It's so obvious someone has snuck into my house—not to steal anything, but to *leave* shopping bags from expensive shops in places where I'd least expect them.

My bedroom closet is like a perpetual Christmas tree, its floor piled high with all these wonderful little packages. Just the other morning I whipped open those big wooden doors and found that the Great Prada Fairy had dropped by, leaving a beautiful black summertime mini just for me! I looked into the sky and whispered a silent and reverent "thank you." Then I snapped out of my blackout—new skirt in hand—and immediately called Visa to assess the damage.

My shopping sprees weren't pretty at all when I was boozing and high, though. Because then I *really* wouldn't remember what kind of financial damage I was doing—day or night. Every afternoon I'd float out to my mailbox and find them full of mysterious packages. Once, apparently, I ordered an entire set of beautiful copper pots and pans from the Home Shopping Network. I've opened Federal Express boxes filled with Cuisinarts, miracle cures, potions designed to give you brand-new, baby-fresh skin in eight days. And I'd cruise through Beverly Hills on High Alert, snapping up everything that moved. Once I bought myself four new pairs of Manolo Blahniks—and got home to find that two of them were duplicates of pairs I already owned. *At $400-plus a pop,* you may be thinking, *I couldn't afford to make that kind of mistake.* Honey, I couldn't either.

I was completely out of control. Once, when I was doing a shoot for *Playboy,* yours truly racked up a cool $32,000 on the American Express bill—entirely on La Perla underwear for me, and champagne for everyone on the entire shoot.

Yes, I bought everything I loved. I was *very* generous with my friends, both women and men. To this day, friends still thank me for that special something I bought them way back when. Most of the time, I just smile—and have no idea what they're talking about. That's the beauty of Alcoholics Anonymous: the more sober you get, the more you regain control of your specific memories. Why did I buy a $2,000 Armani leather jacket for some guy I didn't even like? Go figure.

Did I really need that blender/sunlamp? Did I really need a year's supply of sparkly orange rug cleaner? I was buying cream to combat stretch marks, when I didn't even *have* stretch marks. Why?

Perfliction, baby. *If I buy that, maybe tomorrow morning I'll wake up perfect.*

Here's the trouble, though: Even now that I've regained control of my senses, I still see around me certain things that absolutely *will* make the buyer happier.

There are some purchases I must insist we *all* make in the name of perfection.

When you enlist in Janice's Beauty Army, you must remember that the most important thing is camouflage, darling. But in Janice's unit, you can forget about those putrid green getups. I'm talking about hiding what's just not working.

Let's say you're feeling bloated while trying on those low-rider blue jeans. You have to draw the line and hide what's acting up.

Some among us — ladies, you know who you are — apparently think that the tighter the clothes, the better they fit. *Don't buy a ticket to this Dreamland.* You don't want to look like one of those Pillsbury bread tubes, with the goop just bursting out at every opening. There's nothing quite as disgusting as the type of rolls served up in spandex casing. To quote Randolph Duke, "Spandex can only expand so far." So don't force yourself into the fashion equivalent of a straitjacket.

I also hate those little belly shirts. The other day, I was doing my hike in the canyons near my home when this fortysomething babe came around a bend with abs to die for. How do I know? Because she'd exposed them for all the world to see, presenting them between belly shirt and waistband as if they were a carefully framed work of art. The only thing this woman was missing was a felt-tip marker so she could write across her stomach: *Look at me! Love me! I have perfect abs!* I especially loved her oh-so-innocent *Oh, are you looking at my perfectly toned stomach?* expression. Here's what I'd love to tell that woman: "You worked for those goods, I know. So congrats and good for you. Now buy a whole shirt, and save the spectacle for yourself and your loved ones."

This whole ab encounter reminds me of an evening back a few months ago. One night, after a bout of perfect sex, I was starving from all that exercise. So I went out to a local restaurant and broke my typical protein-only evening diet. I pulled up to the counter and chowed down on some pasta with oil-free sauce. Now, I don't ever, *ever* advise anyone to have pasta in the evening, but I was still glowing from my evening activities, and I couldn't help indulging just a wee bit more.

The following day, fully bloated, I awoke with abs o' *shit* thanks to my late-night pasta treat. Did I go suicidal just because I couldn't wear a little cutoff top to impress my fellow hikers? Nah. This was one of those rare times when I cut myself a break. Every now and then we all deserve a little pasta—and an extra-long T-shirt to cover up the damage.

Back to fashion. Having recovered from my carbo-extravaganza, I soon hit the town in a pair of hot Dior jeans and a tank top. I wear what I want, where I want. I can show up in a coffee shop dressed for a *Vogue* party, and that's okay with me. Ask fashion mavens Sandy Linter or Harry King about the time we were in Florida for a *Vogue* shoot. We were staying at a four-star hotel; there was a tiny coffee shop a block away, though, and there they found me, all dressed up with no place to go. I was staring through the dirty front window when I noticed the two of them outside, laughing at me. *What's so funny?* I wondered. *I look good. Let me live my own fantasy.* I was starring in my own little version of *Cabaret*. Screw them. They were just jealous that Janice was the star.

21

How I've Helped the Famous and Infamous Be More Perfect

So many questions about perfection, so little time.

The other night, I was at an exclusive Bel Air birthday party, feeling totally out of place—as I often do at these soirees.

There was so much fabulousness in the air, it was fucking depressing. So there was only one thing to do: drown out the endless, mindless chatter with the most numbing substance in the ultrachic mansion. I'm not talking about drugs or alcohol. My hooch of choice that night was a *huge* plate of corn chips. I know, I *know*—the fat grams—but what was a girl to do? I needed *something*, and I'd done enough crunches at the gym to crunch a little at the buffet line.

All that loud chewing was pure perfection, though. It drowned out the excruciating silence in my head—that loud and painful nothingness between your ears when you're swimming around a party with no companion to talk to, and nothing but cold stares from all the strangers around you. It's a sound that never fails to make me want to jump out of my skin.

Sure, peace and quiet can be the best gift of all, but, indoors, at an A-list event, silence basically sucks. It's an unmistakable signal: they all think they're more perfect than you.

So I decided to rectify the situation by bringing on da noise. Apparently my junk-food orgy was so fascinating that it caught the attention of none other than Ms. Barbra *"Funny Girl"* Streisand. Suddenly, the singing diva, director, actress, mother, and multimillionaire was in my face. I guess Babs must have been marveling at the sight of a supermodel with the guts to dabble in a product that doesn't get much action in the state of California. It's a miracle I wasn't hauled off to the L.A. County jail right then and there.

Staring wistfully at my greasy corn-chip nirvana, a bewildered Barbra locked her icy blues with my baby browns. She had a painful, pleading look on her face, like that of a woman looking for the answers to life's most important questions.

"What's up, Babs?" I asked midcrunch, and she smiled. I guess she's sick of all those asskissing sycophants who treat her like her shit doesn't stink. I always check my bullshit at the door.

"I know who you are," said Ms. Yentl.

"I know who you are, too," I said *(crunch, crunch, crunch).*

"Janice," whispered Babs, and I stopped chewing. *This sounds serious,* I thought. *Maybe she wants some workout advice.*

"I have to ask you something," Babs continued to whisper. "How in the world can you stay so skinny and eat chips?"

I nodded, swallowed, and gave her the good and bad news. "Swiss Kriss, honey," I shot back. "It's all about laxatives and diuretics." I figured she already knew about canyon walking and yoga.

She was fascinated. "Can you repeat that?"

Opposite: Tina Turner lives. Selling panty hose for a German magazine.

"*Swiss Kriss*. It's a laxative. Once a week—boom—flat stomach. Just stick close to the john, or things could get ugly," I warned her with a smile.

Now I can't say for certain, but Babs was starting to look like she was digging this conversation. I was ready for her to whip out a notepad and start taking notes. I just shook my head. "You know what, Babs? Everything about me is fake—including my intestinal tract."

At this point, Babs laughed so hard that her Evian began to spill on the sleeve of her latest Donna Karan black-brushed gold shirt.

"You should try a good laxative tea—they work, too," I told her, knowing it was my duty to spill the beans. "A few sips in the morning, and . . . thunder!" I said. Now Babs was laughing so hard she was clutching her *own* stomach.

"I can't believe we're having this conversation," she said in that wonderful Brooklyn whine she never really lost. (Thank God.) I was amazed: here was a woman who truly has it all. Yet despite the money, the fame, the work, the acclaim, and the love she's found in the last several years, even *she* still doesn't feel perfect enough.

"Life is a shit sometimes," I told her.

"Janice, you said it," she replied.

Unfortunately, not every icon behaves quite that way.

Some time back, I was on a first-class flight from Los Angeles to Munich with my old friend and flame, photographer Michael Reinhardt. The two of us were arguing about the simple things in a love match— things like territory and control. Mike and I were two alphas; we were always going teeth to teeth with each other that way. It's tough to be in a relationship with someone whose personality is exactly as strong as your own—especially when that means extra-strong.

On that flight, I let him win—but not because I felt like giving up, mind you. He won because I had to take myself out of the fight. Thanks to severe thunderstorms, the plane was rocking. Before too long, the pilot gave us the bad news: "Attention, ladies and gentlemen, I've been informed that we'll have to circle for the next forty-five minutes." At that point the piece of toast I'd consumed earlier that day—along with all the vodka I'd been chugging on the flight—began to churn. So I ran to the bathroom and hurled. Mike just sat there reading his magazine, totally oblivious. (Did he deign to move one leg so I could squeeze past him on my way to the john? I can't remember.)

Afterward, I felt so ill I wasn't sure how I was going to make it back to my seat. When I opened the bathroom door, I looked like death warmed over—but my spirit was suddenly lifted when I locked eyes with this little angel of a girl, standing there patiently waiting her turn.

"Lady, can I help you?" she said in a wee voice, filled with concern. "You all right, lady?" I glanced up to see who mothered this beautiful little girl, but much to my horror discovered the face of gloom. "Get back to your seat and leave her alone!" screamed Ms. Diana Ross to her daughter.

God, no wonder she has such a reputation, my one brain cell thought.

"Doncha talk to my kid," Ms. Ross said, practically shoving me out of the way to go into the bathroom while her kid waited there silently, legs crossed. When your mother's a diva, I guess you have to hold it.

Ah, the kindness of strangers. It's a good thing Ms. Ross didn't ask me for any beauty tips. The first one I would dish out? *Lighten the fuck up.*

Some people who get frown lines actually deserve them.

22.

The Best Beauty Tips Ever

I know you read all the fashion beauty books and magazines that offer a thousand different tips in the name of beauty every single month. I won't mock them—I figure you all know by now that it's a bunch of bullshit, right?

Girls, you honestly don't need to spend millions to turn your already overcrowded bathroom counter into a shrine for the beauty product line of the moment. When it comes to sharing the best in beauty tips, I have it down to a science. Read on, and follow these tips if you want to be . . . totally perfect.

For the Bod

How hard is it to keep your chassis tuned? Ladies, it's *grueling*, I know. My life has been grueling since the 1970s, and it ain't getting any easier. But if you break it down into a million tiny jobs along the way, you might find it easier to cope with what you have to do to stay in control. You've

got to tell yourself what to do. *Hit the gym five or six times a week. (Get over it!) Eat all the greens on your plate. (Don't make that face. I mean all of them, young lady!)*

And you've got to remember what's at stake if you don't. I'm a waistline-is-half-full kind of gal. You can call me pessimistic if you want. But you'll never call me fat.

It's all about what you do with your body—what you put into it, and what you do with all the energy that's waiting to get out of it.

People often ask me: "What do you eat now, Janice?" Here we go:

I start the day with an egg-white omelet. It's a great shot of protein that keeps you feeling full. A little bowl of oatmeal is fine, too—the plain old-fashioned kind, not Maple & Two Tons of Brown Sugar. You *must* eat breakfast. It gives you the energy you need to get the day rolling.

For lunch, I eat anything that flies, swims, or crawls. And I *never* have bread with it. For a snack during the day, I eat plain celery. Why? I work really hard on my body, and I don't want to blow it. I'll also have a small handful of almonds if I'm hungry between meals. I don't mean the whole can, although I do believe it's important to pig out once a week on good stuff that you love. Yesterday, for example, I had a few cookies. Today, I won't. The key is not to abandon your self-control every single day.

You can't go wrong with salmon. Grilled, poached, or chilled, it's great for your body. I eat it once or twice a week. It's good for your brain cells, too—the ones you have left, anyway.

Power Bars, or energy bars, are better than eating a sandwich for lunch, but you can't snack on them relentlessly, thinking that you're doing your bod a favor. They're packed with calories.

I have a huge sweet tooth, and since I stopped smoking it's gotten worse. Giving up alcohol made it even more difficult because alcohol has a ton of sugar. (Remember that the next time you want to go out and have a few drinks and no dinner. You're better off eating a little something and

Opposite: Run a series of these exercises, please.

having only one drink.) Anyway, when I quit smoking and drinking, I did what anyone does: chew, chew, chew. I even did something surprising for a model: I got interested in fabulous baked goods. That's when I noticed my skin was starting to get blotchy. Alas, that's sugar for you. Resist! The saddest thing is when I see someone work out really hard and then later eat a ton of white sugar—or cheese, which works the same way. That's like having liposuction, and then having the pounds sewn right back onto your hide.

For the Fashion-Conscious

For me, exercise and fashion go hand in hand. If you can't feel good about your body, it's going to be harder to feel good about your clothes. And if you hate what you wear to exercise, you're not going to feel good about getting fit. So let's go over what it takes to get yourself *and* your wardrobe in shape.

First of all, exercising is crucial. The PC police will kill me for saying this, but for me the two best motivations to exercise have always been these: the hot guy I've got in bed (and want to keep there) right now, or the next hot guy I'm trying to land. I'll bet you've got one or the other, right, girls? Now close your eyes and think about him for a moment—naked. Doesn't that make you want to get on your feet and work those buns?

I learned as a ballerina that all exercise should start with stretching. I do it every day; if I don't, I feel rusty.

What to wear on a run? Whatever you do, not one of those popular J.Lo–type jogging suits. Here's what I think of them: Hideous! Bleh! Forget 'em. They look as if they were made out of material Motel 6 wouldn't even use for their towels. Can't people just look inside *Vogue* and see what's fashionable? Is that really too much to ask?

I'm not saying we shouldn't wear clothes to relax in. All I wear for hanging out is a pair of stretchy black leotard pants and an oversized T-shirt. Try it. You'll love how loose-fitting they are compared to those tight Juicy jackets. Think classic. Nothing is sexier than a crisp white T. Nothing!

It's not really the best idea to go hiking after lunch wedged into a pair of Dolce and Gabbana pumps. But you'll never catch me taking a quick power walk through Beverly Hills in those dreadful, butt-ugly athletic shoes women all over the country are wearing. Unless you're training for the freakin' Olympics, do yourself a fashion favor: throw those stinkboats

Downtime. No makeup and feeling my groove.

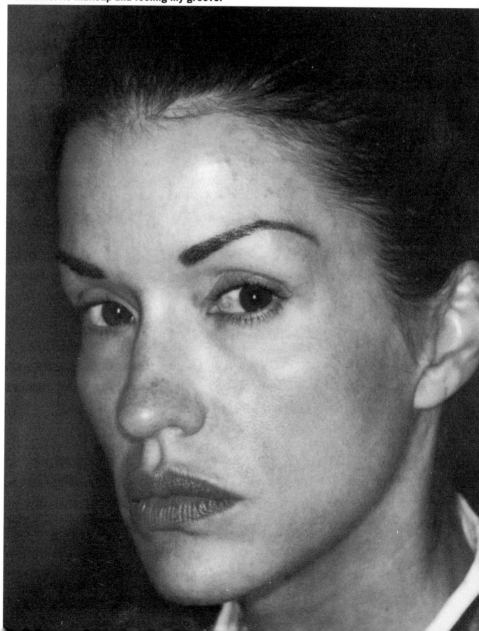

in the trash and get yourself some sexy workout sneaks before you get out there and walk off every meal.

Then again, when you're *not* exercising, you've got to work it. And all I can tell you is this: *please* learn how to walk in high heels. The key to finding good heels is making sure they're secure on your feet. In other words, find your size—or get ready to come face-to-face with the pavement. Believe me, it's worth it to invest in one good pair of four-hundred-dollar Christian Louboutin shoes rather than four pairs of cheap ones from the mall. I discovered Louboutins at a Paris show for Diane von Furstenberg years ago. Fabulous! Carrie Bradshaw wore pink ones for her last date with Mr. Big before he moved out of New York (was he nuts!?) on *Sex and the City*. If they're good enough for both Janice D and Carrie B, well, they're good enough for you, no? They even make your *toes* look hot. Get them in every color if you can! Have the man in your life buy them for you if at all possible. And here's the key: practice walking in them with attitude. Even better, dance in them with abandon. You won't be sorry.

Every woman needs her fair share of fabulous and huge diamond stud earrings. If you can afford the real ones, call me so I can borrow them. If not, buy quality fakes that look real. People will never know in a million years that they're crystal. They'll just think you had a great Christmas. Practice saying things like, "We woke up on Christmas morning and my boyfriend handed me this box that said Harry Winston. Is he a keeper or what?"

Fur or no fur? Here's the whole truth and nothing but: I used to wear leopard back in the day. Did I feel bad because an animal died? Yes, of course. I love animals. I've even worn cheetah. But *heel*, you PETA members: it was a *live* cheetah, which I encountered at a *Playboy* shoot. The cheetah was only supposed to brush up against my body—but he kept getting frisky with me, and every time he did I'd break out into mountains of hives. Why hold a grudge?

I don't own any fur now. I do like the look of faux leopard or faux cheetah, though, especially since both animals are fast and sleek. I just love the vintage look of fur. And, frankly, I think it's okay to wear *old* furs. What's done is done, right?

For the Face

I exfoliate every single day, but for some people that's just too harsh on the skin. See what works for you. I don't believe in those expensive scrubs that you buy over the counter, which are often filled with enough perfume to turn your face purple. Try Quaker cornmeal as an exfoliant for your face, knees, and elbows. It costs pennies, and one box lasts forever.

One must *always* wear fake eyelashes, at least in my world. But I hate those strips of fake lashes that look like you just stepped out of some bad 1970s horror flick. Personally, I swear by individual fake lashes, which come in a little set with glue to place them in between your real lashes for that oh-so-lush look. Now, it's not hard to put them on, so don't skip over this part of the book. You can do it. I know you can! Fake lashes open up the eyes as quickly as I open my legs. (Just making sure you're paying attention!)

Here's how it's done:

1. Give yourself fifteen minutes to apply them, so you don't stress yourself out.

2. Use a little eyelash comb to give your real lashes a quick raking.

3. Look for the gaps in between your real lashes.

4. Using tweezers, dip the tip of the individual fake lash into the adhesive cement and carefully, but firmly, place it in an open space.

5. Adjust them with your finger or the tweezers.

6. If you mess up, just take a breath, remove, and start again.

A quick word on the adhesives involved here: I hate the rubbery-glue type and prefer the cement adhesive, which lasts longer. If you're really careful in the shower, those fakes can last for days.

Some advanced tips on lashes: A small strip of fake lashes looks great in the outer corners of your eyes. Or you can put them in the center of your eyes to make them appear bigger. Remember, with all makeup, less

Not happy with brown hair? Try a perfectly fine red wig on for size . . . POW!

can be more. You are your own best judge of what looks good on you. Be judgmental; hell, be brutal. The best place to check out your face is in the rearview mirror of your car, where you can do it in the most natural light.

If you really don't have time to do individual lashes, then load up on mascara—even if you're afraid people will think you went raccoon wild or haven't slept for a week. But just do the top lashes. Mascara on the bottom has a tendency to melt off on your face in ugly rings. Keep everything up—just like our boobies, we want to lift our eyes.

Mascara can be especially dramatic and beautiful when worn with no eyeliner, too. It's a look I love.

Now, a quick word on the so-called "natural look." There's a big difference between natural with a little makeup (good), and natural like you just got back from working the land. Opt for the first. When I want to look natural, I put a little blush on my cheeks, fill in my eyebrows, toss on two coats of mascara, and then slather on a little bit of lip gloss. All of the above takes approximately twenty seconds.

Let's say you're lacking in expensive eyebrow gel with *Bobbi Brown* on the container. An old toothbrush and a little hairspray will do the trick just as well.

Eyebrows shouldn't be too bushy. I tweeze because I'm into the precision of my look—and besides, you can make mistakes waxing. Afterward, I throw a little body gel on them to get rid of the sting.

Even if you're dead tired, you also need to wash the makeup off your face each night. My good friend Patti Hanson used to turn up for work in three-day-old mascara. Sure, it eventually became a new look, but it came with a price: what happens when you wear the same mascara for days is that eventually your eyelashes become glued together and fall out. So in the interest of saving those suckers, get out the washcloth at night and go to sleep with a fresh, dewy face.

Forget soap.

And fuck Chanel. That skin stuff they sell is overpriced and overperfumed. Just go to the supermarket, get a huge container of plain nonfat yogurt, and lather up. Follow it up with some apple cider vinegar—a great astringent. If pimples form (and they will), pour some more of that apple cider vinegar into a bowl in the sink and give your face a good splash. I've been doing it for years, and I have *zero* pimple scars. If you have a volcano of a zit, don't use your bacteria-hoarding nails to pop it. Take a clean Q-Tip, dab it with fresh lemon juice, and rub it on the zit for a few minutes. The lemon will suck out all the infection.

Every other night I do a facial. I love papaya enzyme exfoliants. You gotta take care of your mug!

It's mandatory to get rid of all unwanted facial hair. You know who you are, ladies! That means those little stragglers on your chin near that mole. And while we're on the topic, all underarm hair must be gone. My ex, Simon Fields, always made me laugh on this one. Whenever he got a glimpse of a woman with excess hair, he'd shudder and say, "Oh—the land that time forgot." Don't *you* forget about it!

As for facial hair on men—how cute is that stuff? I love it when they grunge themselves up, the way Johnny Depp or Brad Pitt do for the occasional film role or a change of seasons. Of course, women don't have that option. Ladies, I repeat: if you think about letting stray hairs go, just think about this: Stephanie Seymour and Kate Moss do not consider stubble a part of their beauty plans.

What do I do? I've tried electrolysis, but it just doesn't work for me. So I've appointed myself to the hair police. I look in my super 10X magnifying mirror to find stray hairs, and rip them out with abandon.

This brings me to sun damage and broken capillaries. Everyone has them—all of the above—but you can't just sit there in front of the magnifying mirror crying, *Woe is me!* There are facials especially designed to get rid of splotching, spotting, and melatonin blotching. I've decided to live my life instead of sitting inside hiding my face. So I ski, and I go out in the sun, and as a result my face takes a beating. I do my best and use sunblock because you've got to be extremely disciplined about sun damage. Trust me—it's an investment in your future.

But I *never* sun my face—ever! And you shouldn't, either. Instead, why not try some self-tanning lotion? I like Clarin's; it gives your face a natural-looking color without you ever having to sit out in the sun, which is just a wrinklefest waiting to happen. The skin comes first, baby: get rid of that winter pale and change your skin color before you work on anything else, like the color of your hair. (And even before you self-tan, remember to exfoliate first, so that you're starting with a clean slate.)

Sometimes your skin may start looking red, and not at all because you let it go to shit. Blotchy skin can be the sign of a bad diet or a medical

Once upon a time in Mexico . . . John Dickinson, ladies.

problem, so check with your doctor or dermatologist. Just one appointment can change it all.

In the meantime, the best thing possible for your skin is to slather Vitamin E, combined with pure aloe vera, all over yourself, from head to toe. It's a cheap and perfect plan for most skin types.

J.D. in the house.

For the Hair

I met hair stylist Nick Chavez on the streets of Paris when he was a hottie-hot male model. I took one look at him and said, "Hey, stud muffin! You busy tonight?" We ended up ripping through Paris together at rapid speed, spreading my paycheck from a Gucci show at the most expensive restaurants in the city.

The debauchery reached quite a fever pitch. One night we were drinking fine wine out of each other's mouths. The next morning, we were late for our meeting with Yves St. Laurent. (We're still really sorry!) The rest is history—except I should mention that Nick became a hairdressing genius, with his own Beverly Hills salon and products on QVC. My hair is in great shape thanks to him (and after all the coloring, highlighting, and processing galore I've endured over the years, I'm lucky I have any left on my head). Nick saved my hair by insisting I use an aloe gel he makes. You can find generic versions almost anywhere: try them. Put it on, throw your hair up into a ponytail, and leave it on all day long or sleep in it. It's a miracle therapy that will revive your luscious locks. (I also love Phyto 7 Hydrating Cream: I rub it on my ends at night before I go to bed.)

Speaking of hair, try to avoid shampooing every single day. Go crazy and skip a day or two. In fact, if you wait until after the weekend, you can go dancing on Saturday night and shake the kind of sexy bed head all the hot models are rocking these days. Remember: raunchy can be hot, too.

For the Mind

Meditate. I've said it before: That's the stuff, for mind and body. Hold this idea in your head: I'm X years *young* (not old). That's how to look at it.

Don't beat yourself up. Worried that you look horrible at the department store? Don't be. Even the world's first supermodel looks awful in that unforgiving lighting!

Have a role model. In my case, I still want to be like Jackie O. I want the dark sunglasses, the basic shift dresses, the hunky Secret Service detail, and a man named Onassis who will take care of me in ways I only dream of at night.

Get a dog. Taking care of another living creature—like my dogs Winston, Carly, and the late Bruno—can be good for your outlook on life and your physical health. (And remember: having to walk your dog means you have to walk your ass, too.)

Stop underestimating yourself. You are adaptable. You are flexible. You can change. Quit tricking yourself into thinking you can't do yoga. You will

Calvin Klein—eat your heart out.

learn the moves. You will find a class you love, in a studio that doesn't reek of curry. You will give yourself a few months to learn, stretch, and grow. Yoga also "opens the chakras," which means letting energy flow through your body uninterrupted. Try it. Trust me.

OTHER UNCATEGORIZABLE WISDOM FROM JANICE

Find a trainer who doesn't smell. Once I had this guy who smelled like garlic. He'd stand right over me while I did sit-ups, and it's a fucking miracle I didn't pass out on the spot. So find someone who makes you feel comfortable—and brushes his or her teeth.

Sleep with bag balm on your feet. It's the stuff they put on cows' udders. Fill your socks with this stuff, slip them on, and I promise you'll wake up in the morning with totally soft footsies.

Don't let your knees look like dried-out piles of hay. Using aloe vera gel, stand upright and let the aloe properties seep into every pore of your body—especially the rough spots like knees and elbows. It's nourishing and hydrating.

Make an avocado mask. Add a little lemon—just make sure you keep it out of your eyes because it will burn. But a mask like this is worth the trouble: it will keep your face, and your hair, smooth and soft.

Have at least one full-length mirror in your house. It might be the only thing around that tells you the truth. Take your clothes off right now, stand in front of the mirror, and examine yourself. Do it in morning or noon light—the harshest light possible. Be tough on yourself. Suck in your stomach and turn sideways. Write down what you want to change about your body because having a written record of it helps. I, for example, hate my saddlebags on the side, my inner thighs, and my lower abdomen. After a close self-examination, I tend to go right out and take a good long walk uphill—because I've suddenly been reminded why I need to sweat. You do the same: remember that image you see in the mirror, and live, eat, breathe, and sweat it till you are where you want to be.

Get on all fours and do those leg lifts you've hated for the past decade. I hate them, too, but I do them. Do side leg lifts if you hate your thighs. If you need to tighten up your lower abs, do those breathing exercises.

Remember: you're not just doing this for a guy. Ideally, you're doing this to feel better about yourself. In the real world, we women all know that we also dress up more for our girlfriends than for the hunk spooning us at night—right? Whatever the case, remember that guys (even the hotties) don't rule the world.

Remember: some of your imperfections aren't your fault at all. Your genes are one culprit; gravity's another. Gravity, especially, sucks. (That's why I'm into surgery, as previously noted.) Call me shallow and vain, but I want to look and feel as young as possible for as long as possible, and I don't see what the hell is so wrong with that.

Give yourself an egg-white facial. Separate the yokes and beat up the whites. Lather it on your face until it dries, which should take twenty minutes or so; then rinse off the mixture. Follow by washing your face with that plain white yogurt to wash away any leftover impurities.

Old makeup brushes begone. If a makeup artist (on a shoot or in a mall) tries to use one on you, slap it right out of their hand and just say no. Who knows where that brush has been? Hands-off is my policy, so that brush better be brand-spanking-new—especially the mascara and the eye shadow applicators. Eye infections are ugly and gross, and don't even get near my mug with that used powder puff unless you're prepared to throw down.

Learn how to walk like you're on a runway. *How, Janice?* Listen and learn:

STEP 1: Eyes straight ahead. Don't ever look down.

STEP 2: Project quiet confidence.

STEP 3: Don't do too much fancy footwork, just long strides.

STEP 4: Don't move too fast.

STEP 5: Keep your chest at a normal level; don't jut it out. Remember, you're not a dancer—and you're not posing for *Playboy*, either.

STEP 6: Think about keeping yourself centered.

STEP 7: Relax. Tell yourself: *I'm not uptight. I'm not stiff.*

STEP 8: Walk like something is for sale that very few can afford.

The best beauty tip of all: Remember, we need to impress *ourselves.* Everyone else? Fuck 'em.

23.

Emotions in Motion

There are times in any girl's life—good or bad—when things just get under your skin. Especially guys. And sometimes, if I'm stressed, those men in my life get an earful from me. Emotional self-control was never my strong suit.

In the old days, when things got tough, all I *thought* I needed was a nice bottle of wine, some coke, or a combination of the two. I spent the better part of two decades de-stressing with booze and drugs, which was par for the course in the modeling world in those days. It was a codependent world, where beautiful beings congratulated one another on their mutual addictions.

What I finally realized, though, was that with drugs and alcohol I couldn't handle the most important job in my life, which was being a good mother. By the 1990s I knew I had to clean up my own act.

Getting sober wasn't easy. I did it with therapy, and by devoting myself to the life-saving, amazing twelve-step program in AA. After many years trying to get sober, I'd been convinced that I just couldn't make any program stick. Part of it was my own stupid pride. I'd go to a group therapy session, look around, and couldn't help but think, "I'm better than all of these losers." Finally my good friend Tony Peck suggested that I might try a twelve-step program. He took me to an Alcoholics Anonymous meeting, and I felt sure that everything would fall into place.

Like many lifelong addicts, I thought that once I "got myself together again," it would be smooth sailing and happy trails. I *wish*. After cleaning up my own mess I was sober, but still completely unhappy—never mind that I was living in this huge mansion in Bel Air with my two children, two dogs, a closet full of Valentino and Versace, a nanny, a career, and the type of functioning lifestyle I had never thought possible.

And yet I still had the urge every night to drink, drink, drink. This killed me because I had devoted myself to kicking booze and drugs, and here I was on the verge of slipping again. It would have been so easy just to pick up that bottle and say, "What the hell? It worked for me all those other years." I've managed to fight off the thirst for years now. But even today, in my darkest moments, I want to drink so badly my entire body is screaming.

Here's what made the difference: a few years ago I picked up a pen and decided to write down my feelings about the abuses I'd suffered as a child, and the life issues I've suffered since. It cost me nothing . . . and everything, all at the same time.

Now, this was a means of recovery I liked. I could purge it all in a healthy way. I knew there was no pulling the wool over this puppy's face anymore. At first I didn't intend to share these feelings with anyone, but all this writing eventually (with the help of my wonderful publisher, Judith Regan) became my first book, *No Lifeguard on Duty*. I slowly realized why I'm here: to share my story, which is a cautionary tale. And I know how lucky I am to be here at all.

Because my leader, Judith Regan, is the world's most ultraconservative boss lady (we're drinking water at her birthday party!), and clearly I am not!

When you're no longer an addict, dealing with the traffic patterns in your brain gets even trickier because you can't fall on those easy fixes. The only thing you have to fall back on is yourself. I'm not always such an easy companion. There are days when my mind screams, *You're nothing but a hideous piece of shit.*

And there's no mute button to push those moments away.

On those days when I'm completely overwhelmed, I go into my bedroom, close the door, and tell the committee inside my head to shut the fuck up. This group that lives inside my brain gangs up on me and screams, *Janice, you're no good. You're less than everyone else. You're not going to get a job, economic doom is around the bend, your kids hate you, and you'll never find anyone to love you.*

Those little damn voices are relentless. But here's the good news: they all work for me. So when things get bad, I just scream: *You're all fired, so get the hell out!*

Janice, honey, you might be wondering, *have you ever talked this over with a shrink?*

I live in California—what do you think?

"Perhaps you have multiple personalities," a Beverly Hills head doc once told me. And when I got done laughing in his well-lifted face, I said, "Me and all my personalities would like to tell you that's bullshit."

Sure, there are plenty of voices in my head. And when they're all speaking up, I silence them by simply asking the Divine Light within me, "Please, let the strongest part of me prevail."

I also tell myself, *I love you.* Then I try to take a deep breath, calm down, and meditate for twenty minutes. When I can, I'll actually leave the house afterward, instead of marinating in my misery.

There's one thing I find I can always do: *Just keep going.* You can, too.

Models aren't the only victims of stress. (*No kidding!*) Check out what happened to me the other day:

I was cruising down Beverly Glen Boulevard after a relaxing two-hour yoga class, feeling fantastic. As I made my way down the pavement, I lightly tapped the horn because some guy was standing up, half out of his car, in the middle of the road, with his door wide open. He looked up and screamed, *"Bitch!"* Then he jumped in the car, gunned it, and pulled out in front of me, nearly causing a massive accident. Suddenly all those good yoga vibes were gone . . . and Ninja Janice was back.

"You have no *idea* what kind of bitch I am!" I screamed. I tailed him; I almost rammed him. I even forced the guy off the road. At that point he began to scream, "You're chemically imbalanced!" (Only in Beverly Hills.)

Phillip Dixon for *Elle* magazine: Hollywood, California. Who says women are lousy drivers?

How did he know?

"You don't know who I am!" he shouted at me. "You'll never work in this town again!"

Now *this* one I couldn't resist. "Honey, you're not the first person who said that—and certainly not the best-looking." Deep down, I kept thinking, *Janice, enough. Enough!*

The real victory, of course, was that I didn't race home and jump into a bottle of pills or booze. I got it out verbally, and that felt pretty damn good. But deep inside I felt like a little girl again, with all the disapproving eyes in the world on her. I started to remember how my father would yell at me and send me to bed without dinner. I would have to sneak downstairs later just to scam a glass of juice. I'd stuff the stress down, sneak out the window late at night, and then wander aimlessly around the neighborhood in the dark, figuring that nothing worse could happen to me outside than could happen to me in my own parents' house.

(See? Even then I knew that walking was a really good way to get rid of what was bothering me.)

Now that I'm in AA, though, I finally have a haven in life—a haven where I can come clean, faults and all, and be welcomed without judgment. "Hi, I'm Janice," I say. "I'm an alcoholic, drug addict, sex addict, candy addict, shopaholic, and all the other aholics in between. Yes, that would be me. But I'm here to tell you that I got to the other side, and now I'm here to be of service to others."

"Hi, Janice," my fellow addicts say warmly, and I feel at home.

I don't want to come off like some Alcoholics Anonymous warrior. But my friend Tony, and others, recognized that this was the ideal program for me because a good way to get out of my own head is to be of service to the community, society, and mankind. It can be as simple as smiling at someone at a traffic light. I just want to spread the warmth. At the grocery store, I'll tell someone, "That's a very nice way you wear your hair." Who doesn't want to hear one nice thing about themselves each day?

I tell everyone I know to try the same thing themselves. It feels just as good to give as it does to receive—sometimes even better.

The other thing that feels good to me is *staying busy*. Personally, if I'm not multitasking, I go insane. I can walk the dog in Gucci stilettos, stretch in my workout clothes, and talk on my cell all at once. If you need stress relief, stretching can be your friend. Harboring stress is the worst possible thing for your body and soul: keep too much inside, and you'll end up acting it out in other ways.

So try everything you need to work it out until you find what works. Tap dance, talk fast, work hard, play hard. Just get it out. As Diana Vreeland once said, "The most extraordinary thing you can do is just feel the power of the waves."

Waves are great, and sometimes I let the ones inside me roar because I know one thing: it's okay to be vulnerable today. And tomorrow. And the next day.

24.

Compulsives Anonymous

I work like a demon when it comes to everything—self, children, dogs, house, boyfriends, and friends. I need my own madness in order to keep the career going. At a certain point, it has less to do with brains and more to do with nonstop drive. My mantra is, "Just do something, and do it as hard as possible."

But it sucks to be this compulsive. I *suffer* for beauty, for work, for love; I'm always moving at 500 miles per hour. My mind knows no speed limit.

In my blindness to keep pushing forward, I often wonder: *What makes me so compulsive? And is it bad for me to be this motivated when I'm trying to maintain an optimistic worldview?*

Here's one thing I've learned: It was my father who made me this compulsive. Whenever I'm left to my own devices—when I'm not out there trying to break down walls—all my abuse issues come to the forefront. I still hear his ugly voice constantly in my ear: "You're not good enough. You'll never amount to anything." After living through the storms of my childhood, you might think I'd find tranquillity as an adult who knows it all. I wish it were so.

Just knowing isn't good enough. Just understanding *why* doesn't make me happy. Now the problem isn't someone else telling me that awful stuff. The problem is *me* telling myself I'm not good enough, and I can do that on a daily basis for one simple reason: I'm never satisfied.

At times, of course, I am content—when I go out on the town wearing a beautiful black cocktail dress with dope evening shoes, or when I dine at a lovely restaurant

But that happiness is fleeting. Because the minute I go home and take off the threads, my mind races and demands, "Now what?"

The need to keep moving forward brings me right back to that ballet class I took as a child. I was never satisfied with the basic ballet positions the school taught me. First, second, third position—give me a break. I wanted to expand upon them, improve them, to create new positions that came from *me*.

As a teenager I was a skinny nothing, so I rode my bike five miles every day to the beach to make sure my legs changed shape (it worked). "Get your ass moving, Janice," I berated myself every time I slowed down. When that stopped working, I enrolled in karate classes, even though some of the older guys hurt me when we sparred together because they were so much bigger. "Flying side kicks will make for a firm butt," I told myself to get past the pain. Was it obsessive? You bet my increasingly cuter ass it was.

When you're an obsessive kid that way, let me tell you—you never shake it.

The other day, when I popped into the Starbucks by my house, I overheard a woman in front of me complaining to her friend, "I never lose any weight, even though I'm on my treadmill for an hour a day and take a yoga class," she said. "I just don't know what I'm going to do. I'm ready to kill myself."

"Excuse me, ladies," I interrupted, addressing the potential treadmill suicide. "Can I just interrupt to say I overheard your entire conversation, and you look fabulous."

I meant it, despite the fact that she was a large blonde woman far from the dewy, spindly model type with 0 percent body fat. She was a chunky chick by most standards—but she was still completely stunning. That's why I felt the need to pay her a compliment.

Of course, she refused to take it that way. "How can *you* possibly say I look good," she retorted. "Look at you!"

I took a deep breath and reminded myself that this woman wasn't angry with me, but with herself. "You know what?" I offered. "Why not try to find some balance in your life? I've led a life of fucking-binging-purging-working-out-until-you-drop. Believe me, I didn't feel the way you think I felt when I looked the way you want to look."

"Like *you* ever feel bad about yourself," her friend muttered.

"Honey," I responded, bringing it down one level to a place where we could all relate—supermodel to model woman. "Look, I've got my *period* right now. I've been so bloated for two days that I think I might explode. I'm on the verge of hemorrhaging, but I still can't miss one day of yoga class. Because I'm just as obsessive as you are." The women fell silent. Now we were on a level playing field.

"And as for not liking myself? Let me just say that when I'm up five pounds with water bloat and blood, I have so much self-loathing going on that I want to throw myself in front of a Mack truck. And the only thing that keeps me from going through with it is the idea that I'll miss, get clipped, and then be scarred for life. You know, one more thing to worry about," I said, fishing around my Prada bag for my coffee money.

By this point, the women were in hysterics.

"Clearly, you ladies better not argue with me anymore because I'm hormonal, but my fucking yoga teacher just told me that I need to learn how to embrace the hormones. Come to terms with them."

"Fuck him," said the first woman.

"Exactly," her friend affirmed. "Screw him, in the most Zen way."

How compulsive am I about having this fantasy life I've created in my own mind?

Well, a few weeks ago my loving son Nathan didn't get me a Mother's Day card or a present. *Fuck that behavior!* I was really hurt because Nathan is growing into a young man now, and he's old enough to know better. Apparently his father didn't even suggest that he buy his own mother a lousy card. In my mind, he should have insisted: "Nathan, do something nice for your mother." Hell, I'm always telling him, "Give your sister a hug." Kids need direction.

So I stewed about that for *weeks*. For the most part I kept it to myself, but I was mad.

And then I realized something: in my own compulsiveness, I was trying to write a script for everyone in my life. I was trying to get them all to step up and fit themselves into my little vision of a perfect world. I push my kids just as hard as I push myself, and I tell myself it's because it's the right thing to do—but sometimes I realize it's because I'm still working out issues of my own.

I've got to stop that. We *all* have to stop that. And I'm trying. Really.

Sabotage: We All Do It

Back in the late 1980s, on a Perry Ellis shoot, I became fast friends with another model who had a serious coke habit.

"You need help," I told her through my own drug haze, perfectly aware that I was talking not just to her, but to myself. Well, my friend—we'll call her Susan, for purposes of not ratting her out—was smart enough to get herself into rehab that December. At the time, rehab was becoming quite the chic place to spend the Christmas holidays. If you were too young, too fast, and too rich, the way to ring in the New Year didn't involve debauchery at some tropical island, or even running up a billion dollars up and down Madison Avenue. For once it was by doing what was actually good for one's health and sanity. Who would have thought?

The minute a hot model announced that she would be "rehabbing," though, the shit usually hit the fan—the *corporate* shit, anyway. First of all, Susan's agent didn't think "a holiday break" would be a good thing, because he knew he could book her straight through to the New Year—racking up more money for her and more commissions for himself. For Susan, of course, that would just mean more opportunities to stress out and get wasted. But what did he care? What he certainly *didn't* want was his racehorse hanging out where the getting-to-know-you, let's-make-a-deal cocktail of choice was Crystal Light or cranberry juice. Susan's bookers also went apeshit, warning her that she'd lose her spot in the modeling pecking order if she dropped out of sight even for a few weeks.

What was a girl to do? Well, Susan was strong enough to tell them all to go to hell. "Happy holidays, you assholes!" she said. "I'm going to rehab!"

After clearing all the vodka and coke out of her condo, she checked herself into a lovely California facility filled with glamorous movie stars, rockers, and other beautiful people looking for a better way. Her days were spent in group counseling sessions, where she talked about her crappy mother and the guy who had raped her at age thirteen. For the first time, Susan was actually talking about the things she'd been burying under layers of designer clothes, pounds of makeup, and tons of drugs.

The fashion industry, of course, didn't come to a grinding halt just because one babe went AWOL for eight weeks. But there was one glitch for Susan. She was forced to miss one final Perry Ellis shoot before the end of the year—and the rehab offered no furlough for strutting your stuff in the Big Apple. Perry Ellis cancelled her contract and refused to give her the promised Christmas bonus she'd planned to use to pay for re-hab. Her agent left her several frantic messages explaining that she was also seriously pissing off Calvin and Ralph, who wanted her to do holiday shows, and might not want to "deal with her" in the coming year if she didn't come through.

I have to hand it to Susan: she finally told the rehab people not to give her any more phone messages. She was sticking with her plan—and if she had to work at a convenience store when she got out, well, so be it. She would wear polyester and be clean. End of story.

Cut to February. Susan was out of rehab, clean, sober, and feeling great. An exec from one of the major fashion labels promptly invited her out to dinner at the Ivy in Beverly Hills to discuss future contracts. (So much for working that register!) It turns out he was willing to negotiate a nice long contract with Susan, and to celebrate he had a wonderful idea.

"I want to order the most expensive bottle of wine on the list," he announced.

Now, this man knew Susan wasn't drinking: his company was one of the fashion houses that had wanted her while she was in rehab, and her agent had been honest with them all.

"But I'm just out of r-rehab," Susan stammered to this exec, not quite believing that anyone would want her to slide back into the pit. "I'll take a cranberry juice, and we can toast that way."

The exec just shook his head and ordered the $200 bottle of wine. When it came to the table, he went through the whole vino ritual: sniffing the cork, swirling it around in his glass, and tasting it. He even took great pains to pour Susan her glass, and insisted that they toast. "Who cares about sobriety?" he said. "You were much more fun before rehab."

Susan turned to the waiter, politely handed him her glass of wine, and said, "I'll have a cranberry juice." The exec shrugged and chugged down the rest of the bottle.

Stories like this just go to show how many people in this business (and in life) don't want you to have it all together, and couldn't care less about your efforts to stay sane. That's why it's so important to police yourself, and not let these assholes seduce you back to those dark places you know aren't good for you.

(By the way, my friend refused to sign an exclusive deal with this moron—which just made him want her more, treat her better, and shove more money at her than she ever thought was possible. She decided to use the cash to help a friend go to rehab. It only seemed right.)

I've seen it all in this business. There was one B-movie starlet—I can't tell you her name—who met me at an audition in this New York studio that smelled like dog shit. She took one look at me and said, "You know, if I were you, I wouldn't even try out for this movie. I hear all the character wears is a G-string and stilettos."

"What do you mean? Don't go in for the audition?" I said, sweetly. I wanted to see how far this bitch would go to sabotage me.

"It could ruin your career," she said, flashing me a smile I'd seen on television and in the movies.

"Honey, I've made a living for years going naked. A G-string will be a nice change of pace," I replied. "I guess you shouldn't go in, either. After all, how can you wear a G-string after just having a baby last month?"

"I didn't have a baby!" she stammered.

"Oh, I'm sorry," I said, staring at her stomach. She just slinked away.

Later on, a friend called me up to tell me that the starlet in question had pulled this trick many times in the past. She ran into my friend at another audition and warned her not to read for what was really going to be "a soft porn film." In the end none of us got the role, which made me happy; at least you-know-who with her backstabbing ways wasn't rewarded for her treachery.

A few months later, I ran into Ms. Starlet at another casting call. This time she was talking to a beautiful young girl. "They'll want you to do all these horrendous things in this movie," she whispered. "You should just get out of here now." Would it ever end?

"You know, Janice. They have really early calls on this movie," she tried to warn me. But now she was dealing with the Big Dog.

"Well, if they want me in before ten, that's good. I'll just be getting in from the night before—I can just swing over to the studio," I said. Scumbag Starlet just shrugged and walked off.

The last time I saw her working was on a late-night cable movie that was more about ass than class. "Who did she beat out?" I wondered out loud. "She must have told the three other hookers who showed up to audition they'd have to work for free."

This kind of sabotage may be bad—but self-sabotage is worse. I was re-minded of this recently when one of my friends and I were salivating over the dessert menu at a chic little Beverly Hills eatery. My friend just sat there moaning that she needed to lose thirty pounds. "I really shouldn't have dessert," she said. "But how bad can a little sorbet be?" I told her we'd split something; I knew dessert wasn't the real problem here.

"How did you start gaining in the first place?" I asked her. And she poured out a truly sad story: not only was her fiancé fucking around with a younger girl, now he was going to marry the little Twinkie—who, inci-dentally, worked in the local ice cream parlor. I kid you not. And here was my brilliant girlfriend, with a Ph.D. in psychology, spending her Sat-urday nights curled up with her new best friend: Sara Lee.

Why do so many of us sabotage our chances to get to the next level of happiness? Because some bitch or some jerk has managed to convince us that we don't deserve it anyway. I know because I've been there. You can call me the Queen of Fucking Things Up on Purpose.

My problem revolved around a man, too, but it's not what most peo-ple think. He was my first role model. He was a pedophile. And he was my father.

Here was a man who beat me on a daily basis because I wouldn't ac-commodate his sexual demands. It set me up for a lifetime of feeling bad—which I thought gave me carte blanche to wreck my own life in the most boring ways possible, including booze, drugs, and inviting the wrong men to share my 300-thread-count sheets.

To some degree, I'm sure, we've all been there. We do moronic things we know aren't good for us, but we can't seem to stop ourselves. There's something liberating about being so bad—at least that's how I felt as I tried to get through the 1970s and 1980s. It was far from a per-fect lifestyle—hell, it wasn't even halfway decent when I think about it now.

The one thing I managed to avoid was overeating. Instead I did co-caine to feel better, and when that didn't work, I dove headfirst into tons of plastic surgery. When that didn't work, I shopped until I dropped, and nearly keeled over when I got my credit card bills. When the buying spree didn't work anymore, I filled the empty spots with sex, sex, and more sex. And even when I was held in the strongest and most comforting of arms, I couldn't find a moment's peace. After too much coke, too much plastic, and too many $10,000 American Express bills, I was still thinking about my father.

Now I've learned to fill myself up by walking in the light—which I know sounds all deep and spiritual, but it works. It's part of my own personal twelve-step program, which is what made me want to write this book in the first place. I want to encourage women and men of all shapes, ages, and forms to try to reach *forward* instead of backward. I may still hear my father's voice in my ear every day, but I keep busy, keep driving, keep fighting. My first book was subtitled *The Accidental Life of the World's First Supermodel*, but I probably should have called it *The Driven Life of the World's First Supermodel*.

Here's what I want to share with you:

If you can just put your hand out and embrace something new, the good in your life will start to outweigh the bad. The best way to think about the future is to think of an expectation that's so far-fetched you can't even really imagine it happening for you. It's the opposite of sabotage: it's shooting for a future that's so bright you can't even imagine it. Why not believe in magic—even if you're in your forties, with two kids and a mortgage you're not sure how you're going to pay?

Don't you still deserve something extraordinary? I know I do—because of my past, and in spite of it, too.

Little changes work, too. For instance, I try to learn ten new words a day. I pick up the dictionary and find ten words I don't know, write them down, and then use them throughout the course of the day. I think it makes me more interesting. Not so bad for a dumb model, eh? You might eat right at one meal, or put down a drink. Baby steps.

The other day Rene Russo called me from location in upstate New York. It was the weekend, and the snow was coming down hard on her perfect strawberry-blonde locks. But on the other end of the line my long-time friend was sobbing.

"Honey, what's wrong?" I asked her. I love this woman—I couldn't stand to hear her so sad.

"I just read No *Lifeguard on Duty*," she wailed. "And I want you to know, Janice, that it meant so much to me." Rene went on to explain how the book confirmed something she'd always felt about me, ever since we'd modeled together back in the day.

"Your talent hasn't even arrived yet," my beautiful friend told me. "You haven't even cut your teeth yet. I believe in you so much."

Now I was crying. (Which ruins those individual lashes, by the way.)

It was good for my heart, though. Rene and I have daughters the same age; we're both Aquarian women who have been through it all and are still standing strong. Look at us today: Rene is one of Hollywood's hottest actresses, and I'm a bestselling author. Two models who probably never dreamed we'd make it to our age intact—never mind still working, still succeeding. It took a few changes along the way, sure. But here's a tip from Hollywood: every great script goes through rewrite before the story hits the screen.

There's always time to rewrite your own script. Just alter your approach: change your diet, your love life, your work life; change your body, your soul, your future. It's all in the approach you take. You can start by refusing to label yourself today the way you did yesterday. You don't need to be "the fat girl" anymore, or "the dumb wife" whose husband cheats on her. I used to call myself "an old whore" or "a bitch," until someone suggested to me that I stop putting myself down like that. In other words, I changed my approach.

Guess what? It worked.

25.

The Perfect Ending

When I'm having good sex, I *scream.*

It's not just the sex—not usually, anyway. It's because I am a passion addict. I clean house the same way: way too fast and sometimes too hard. I just can't stop myself. And I was the same way with this book. My objective was to share my feelings about how we all mess up our lives trying to be perfect—and I had to take it all the way. I couldn't just share a little bit. I had to share hard, yell it from the rafters.

In our quest to be perfect, we often hide our true feelings or wrap them in sweet-smelling packages. This is why I want to create a perfume someday and skip the silly French labels. I would call my scent Sexy Bitch. The slogan could be: "Wear it and get laid." At least I'd be telling the truth—and that's as perfect as it gets.

(And did you just catch me calling myself a bitch again? Do I contradict myself? So sue me.)

These days I live just as hard as I did back then, but in a good way. I wake up, leap out of bed, and let the light flood my bedroom—and my soul. I get down on my knees next to my bed and thank God for allowing me to start another day with a clean slate. I know now that I don't have to be totally perfect. Of course, I know that you can do anything with a clean slate, good or bad. It's up to you to mark it in a good way, or mar it forever. The choices are endless; they're intimidating; but they can be inspiring.

And how do I feel about perfection these days? Well, don't hate me, but I'm loyal to my cause. Call me crazy, but I'm still willing to make myself a guinea pig. The other day, I had a substance called Artefill injected into the various little wrinkles around my face—the ones that Botox just doesn't seem to be able to handle. They tell me Artefill is the better Botox. Of course, the process of getting puffed hurts a little bit—they've never made a needle that feels good—and afterward your face swells a bit, like you've just been attacked by killer bees. We'll see if it holds up as well as the rest of me.

But I'm also learning to relax, in the hope that new lines won't form. These days, even when I step back into the modeling game, I take it all in

The two Lucies singing along with the radio. Bel-Air, California, 1998.

stride. To tell you the truth, I love being on the other end of the camera almost as much as I do modeling, and my photos have appeared in hundreds of national publications.

I don't even sweat the bad moments. A few years ago, for example, I was standing on a dock in Key West with about $20,000 worth of camera equipment strapped on my body. Well, it was too much (isn't this business always too much?), and I felt myself drifting backward under all the weight. Suddenly I was off the dock and in the water—laughing my head off.

My equipment was destroyed, and the girl posing for the cover of Italian *Cosmo* looked suddenly skittish, like maybe I was going to blame her.

"Honey, jump in with me," I cried, and she did.

A few minutes later, I was on my cell phone calling an ex-boyfriend who lived in the area. "Can you bring me a camera?" I laughed, picking seaweed out of my hair.

Moral of the story: Seaweed is a great conditioner.

Almost every single day, I try to teach my daughter, Savvy, a little something about how fabulous her life is. I tell her that she's gorgeous, that she's smart, that she can be anything she wants to be and more. I'm desperate to make sure she feels secure with her life—so desperate, in fact, that whenever I lose my temper (like any other nervous parent), I always come back and apologize. "You're still gorgeous and smart," I'll say sweetly. "But get those wet socks off the bathroom floor right now,"

I worry about my daughter, though. I worry about body image in a world where J.Lo's muscle tone is fodder for *National Enquirer* stories. I hate it when the tabs do that kind of thing to women; after all, we all have our off-days, our things we'd rather hide. What does it say to my daughter when even the hottest of the so-called beautiful *things du jour* isn't perfect enough?

(Of course, I loved it when the tabs did the same thing to Jerry Hall back in the 1990s—because she *did* have some extra flab in her glutes. The photographer caught her flaunting her ass next to some tropical beach house Mick bought her. At the time, I guess it didn't bother me so

much because Savvy was too young to know the difference between Jerry Hall and Tom & Jerry.)

Now, though, I worry. "Is J.Lo fat?" Savvy asked me, her beautiful eyes wide. This was one talk I knew she'd remember.

"No, honey," I said, directing her gaze up to the smile on Jenny-from-the-Block's mug. "She looks really happy, doesn't she? That's the only thing that matters."

My daughter seemed satisfied, but I still had to wonder what society wants from women—including little women like Savvy, who are just coming up in a world that likes to knock us down for sport.

Of course, life isn't always perfect. How do I deal with my children being able to pick up either of my books and hear the randy details of their mom's past? I have to find some sort of positive way around this.

The other day my teenage son gave the keys to our new house to his friends to use while I took them to Hawaii for a blowout spring break surprise. Yes, while I was treating the kids to a week in paradise, seven of Nathan's male friends decided to party down at Chez Janice. They thought I'd never figure it out, of course; at my age, could my brain really be up to speed?

These kids had no idea who they were dealing with.

When I got home, I found one of their empty vodka bottles in my trash. "Nathan!" I yelled. "I want to talk to you. Now!"

My son knew there would be consequences. I'll admit it, I felt a little bad for him; peer pressure's a bitch. And I'm sure he thought I was, too, when I hauled him and his seven good-time guys into my living room the following day (after I calmed down). "Boys," I told them, "Here's the deal. When you do something bad, you have to give something good back to the universe."

They just looked at me like I'd snapped. That was just too bad for them.

Opposite: Perfection achieved. Mark Giard, 2003.

"Next weekend, the eight of you are going to volunteer at a homeless shelter and help serve food. Where are you going to get the food, you ask? Well, part of it's going to come from a food drive you'll be conducting in the next few days." I said. "By the way, the homeless people don't need vodka, so you can leave that off your shopping list."

After some grumbling, the eight party hounds hauled their little cookies down to the shelter. After spending an entire day there, Nathan came home, gave me that soft little-boy glance I miss so much, and said, "You know, Mom, we do have it pretty good."

I nearly passed out. It was a perfect moment.

26

The Kind of Love That Makes My World Perfect

Hang on. I saved the best for last: Love.

Here we go.

Last night, I lost my wallet. I was frantic: that little wedge of leather holds half my life between its folds. I was flipping out so badly I almost swallowed my tongue. Among other things, the pictures in my wallet were *fabulous*—driver's license included. It had taken three hours at the DMV for me to take that photo. I didn't care if that scrawny, prison-record-looking kid behind the counter had two hundred people in line. I made them take about sixty shots until I was satisfied. No one says no to Janice, babe.

And now, after all that effort, suddenly it was lost. I was a shambles. After finishing my freakout, I went back to the pet store where I'd dropped off my dogs for grooming, and said a silent prayer that I'd find my wallet.

Then I ran into Eddie, a friend of mine from the days (and nights) when I used to hang out with model Beverly Johnson. At first Eddie didn't spot me—he was talking on his cell with his psychic; how L.A. is that?—so I grabbed the phone away from him.

Before I could say a word, the psychic said, "Hello, honey. I think you need to go back to your car. You'll find what you're looking for between the seats." Now, *this* was service. I flew back to the car like I was running for my life, jumped inside, and pushed the electronic seat adjuster. As I pushed it back, my wallet practically fell into my hands.

Obviously this was too big an opportunity to pass up. I hauled ass back into the store. "Eddie, would you hand me your phone again? I'm shellshocking here."

Before he could even hand me the cell, I grabbed it. "Hello, is this still the psychic? Thank God! Now, what about my relationships? When will I find true love?"

She said, "For that you will have to look into yourself."

See! What I've been preaching all along. Who needs a palm reader?

The truth is, when it comes to love, I'm still walking around with the feelings of a sixteen-year-old girl who's just coming into her own hormones. I hope it doesn't fade, either, because I like the feeling—and you just can't fake this kind of stuff. Next year I might write another book called *Fucking Great at 48*—and it won't (necessarily) be about what's happening in bed, but what's in my head and my heart.

Of course, when I spot a guy and I start to fall in love, I think all the typical girl's thoughts—thoughts that have everything to do with why I wanted to do this book: *Am I wearing the right thing? How do my tits look in this shirt? Is the thirteen inches of makeup on my face too much? Should I really have spent three and a half hours in the bathroom this morning to get ready? The hair extensions, the fake lashes, the concealer, the heels—is it enough?*

Am I perfect enough?

Then one day I realized: *Everything about me is fake . . . and I'm perfect.*

This is my favorite photograph ever taken—period.

I hope you'll all get there, too, the way I did—with luck, without all the trouble it took me to get there. Just breathe and be fabulous. Put out a vibe that says you're the best, and before you know it you'll believe it, feel it, and *be* it. That's how I've gotten through life—it ain't perfect, but it works.

Treat yourself well. I don't care who or what you are in this lifetime, get out of the house on Saturday night. Put on your trashiest outfit, shortest shirt, hottest fishnet stockings (with seams), and find the perfect pair of dancing shoes. I buy mine at a place called I Love Shoes in Beverly Hills. I love the spiked Italian stilettos that you can dance in without ending up at the chiropractor.

But remember that life isn't just one big party. A few weeks ago, I went on a camping trip to pump myself up for my book tour. I'll never forget it: first thing in the morning the birds were so loud I was almost gasping. It was so beautiful—like being in Heaven. I awakened with the sun and took an hourlong walk into the woods, and suddenly I realized I was at peace with the world—because my head was clear and my ass was hovering well above my kneecaps. What more could I possibly want from this life?

People ask me, "Janice, tell me one more time—how did you get yourself together?"

My reply is simple: "Who says I'm together?"

My mantra used to be *Whatever will be, will be.* These days I've replaced that with something much better: *It is what it is what it is . . .*

How do I keep it together? I try to stay connected to the important people in my life, the ones who keep me focused and grounded. I try to be diligent about my routine maintenance, scrubbing, exfoliating, tweezing, plucking, and primping—and I do it not just because it's business, but for myself. And I work just as hard at taking care of the inside as I do the outside. When I stare into the mirror, I like the person who looks back at me—at least most of the time, which seems good enough. I know it's her imperfections that make her perfect.

When I look into her eyes, she appears to be about sixteen years old in spirit, but with the body and the mind of someone who has been put through the wringer. Some people call that maturity. I call it late blooming. I may be the latest bloomer of all.

These days I feel like today's Mary Tyler Moore, only happier and sans that stupid fucking beret.

One thing that keeps me going, I know, is just pure *energy*. I'm writing this after getting home from an AA meeting where I was speaking with a woman who had been sober for twelve hours. Notice I didn't say *only* twelve hours because every one of those hours was a victory that woman snatched from the bottleneck of defeat. My role there is to be of service and help the next person, the way I was helped myself. And that's another thing that keeps me sane.

I certainly don't have all the answers. Maybe I don't really have *any* answers. All I can tell people is that you should live your life in gratitude for this day, whatever it brings, because that is perfect enough.

My path is one of the spirit (loving life), the mind (AA), the body (yoga), and the soul (my kids, and what love I can find). I try to make sure my own side of the fence is clean. I'm not a warrior about it. There are days when it gets kind of messy, but then I work extra-hard to clean it up. I've gathered enough self-respect to know that I deserve it.

Is all that perfect? Hell, no.

It is what it is what it is . . .

Hang on a minute. What? You thought I was done? Please.

So a few months ago, I'm at this lavish *Vanity Fair* party in Beverly Hills, celebrating the genius of filmmaker Billy Wilder, who directed one of my favorite films—*Some Like It Hot*. Speaking of hot, the crowd was strictly A-list, and it included Mr. Mick Jagger. Didn't he used to be some famous rock star?

I wasn't pregnant Janice anymore. I was size-four, yoga-toned, head-on-straight, skin-glowing, hair-flowing Janice (thanks to three hours in the chair and enough hair care and self-tanning product to keep an entire factory running for a year). I was looking hot, if I do say so myself, in a red, low-cut, va-va-Valentino dress. Eyes, and D-cup fake breasts, were popping everywhere.

Once again, Mick snubbed me completely.

That's a rock star's love for you.

He didn't even waltz up to say hello. (Maybe he doesn't go for ex-lovers anymore.)

In the past, I would have let a stream of curses fly. Instead, I pivoted on my Blahniks and did something shocking—especially for someone who's spent her whole life trying to make everything around her perfect.

I let it fucking go.

I didn't get mad. Instead, I just walked up to someone far more interesting than Mick. Who? Mr. Billy Wilder himself. Soon we were deep into a conversation about everything in sight: art, photography, the cinema. Billy and I made love with our minds, and it was beyond perfect.

Glancing at Mick on the way out, I felt not a shred of anger.

Who cares anymore? I thought. For me, this is progress.

As I drove away in my top-down Mustang, my hair being undone by the Santa Anas, I wondered for a moment why I felt so different that night.

Duh. Because I'm *happy* these days.

I'm a model. I've spent a lot of time putting on a happy face. But I'm not faking it anymore. I know how much effort it takes to conjure up one of those fabulous fake smiles. Now, when the world's first supermodel tosses out her cover-girl grin, she means it. It's backed up by knowledge, experience, and guts.

What could be more perfect?

Oh, and in case you're reading this, Mick? I'm Janice, babe. The original.

Don't forget it.

Don't underestimate it, either.

Index

Page numbers in *italics* refer to illustrations.